Elevate Your Life

Elevate Your Life

Sloane Montgomery

Contents

Introduction: The Power of Questions

In life, we are often told that having the right answers will lead to success. We focus on what we know, seeking to gather facts, accumulate knowledge, and master specific skills. Yet, what if the key to true personal and professional growth wasn't found in the answers we seek, but in the questions we ask?

Questions are incredibly powerful. They ignite curiosity, challenge assumptions, and open doors to new possibilities. By asking ourselves meaningful questions, we begin to examine our lives more deeply. We start to reflect on our choices, habits, beliefs, and goals. This introspection helps us identify what's working, what's not, and where we can improve.

Think about the moments in your life when you felt stuck, unsure of what to do next. What made the difference? Often, it wasn't just receiving advice from others or finding a magical solution. It was asking the right question—one that made you think differently or see your situation from a new angle. That's the real magic of questions: they transform the way we view ourselves and the world around us.

In this book, we will explore how asking the right questions can elevate both your personal and professional life. By breaking down key areas of growth, we'll guide you through a series of thought-provoking questions designed to enhance self-awareness, build resilience, and sharpen your focus. These questions will act as a catalyst for growth, helping you make more informed and intentional decisions.

Each chapter will cover a specific theme, whether it's discovering your purpose, mastering time management, or developing leadership skills. Within each theme, the questions will be tailored to uncover insights that allow you to take meaningful action. This book isn't about quick fixes or superficial changes; it's about fostering lasting transformation by getting to the heart of what really matters.

Asking the right questions is not a one-time event; it's an ongoing process. Life is constantly evolving, and so are you. That's why the questions in this book are designed to be revisited. The more you engage with them, the more they will grow and evolve with you.

By the end of this journey, you will have gained not only a deeper understanding of yourself but also the tools to continue asking the kinds of questions that lead to greater clarity, fulfillment, and success.

So, let's begin. Ask yourself: What would my life look like if I started asking better questions today?

The answers might just surprise you.

Part 1: Elevating Your Personal Growth

{ 1 }

Chapter 1: Discovering Your Purpose

Understanding the Concept of Purpose
What is purpose? It's a word that often carries significant weight, yet its true meaning can seem elusive. Purpose goes beyond the surface-level goals we set for ourselves or the daily tasks that fill our schedules. It's a deep, intrinsic force that gives our lives direction, meaning, and fulfillment. To discover your purpose is to uncover the very reason you get out of bed each morning, the driving force behind your actions, decisions, and aspirations.

Understanding purpose begins with recognizing that it is personal. No two people will have the exact same purpose, just as no two people will have identical life experiences. Your purpose isn't something you can simply copy from someone else or find in a quick internet search. It's an evolving understanding of what gives your life meaning, what you contribute to the world, and how you align your actions with what matters most to you.

Many people think of purpose as a singular, all-encompassing mission. They believe that once they've "discovered" their purpose, everything will fall into place, and life will become effortless. In reality, purpose is more fluid. It may shift over time as you grow, learn, and experience different stages of life. Your purpose at age twenty may differ from your purpose at forty, and that's perfectly normal. What remains constant is the need to continuously reflect and re-evaluate how your current life aligns with your deeper sense of meaning.

One of the most common misconceptions about purpose is confusing it with short-term goals. While goals are important for motivation and achievement, they don't necessarily reflect your deeper sense of why. For example, a goal might be to get a promotion at work or to run a marathon. These are admirable aims, but they are often tied to external outcomes. Purpose, on the other hand, is about your internal compass—it's the "why" behind the goals you set. If your purpose is to help others, a promotion at work may align with that if it allows you to positively impact your team. If your purpose is to challenge yourself physically and mentally, running a marathon might fulfill that purpose. Purpose gives meaning to your goals and connects them to something larger.

To begin understanding your purpose, it's essential to reflect on your values and passions, two key components we'll dive into more deeply later in this chapter. Ask yourself: What drives me? What gives me energy? What do I feel is my unique contribution to the world? These questions will help you start identifying patterns in your life—times when you felt most alive and connected to something greater than yourself. Purpose often lies in these moments, waiting to be uncovered.

Discovering your purpose isn't a one-time event. It's an ongoing process of self-reflection, evaluation, and growth. You may not find your exact purpose immediately, and that's okay. The act of asking yourself these deeper questions is already a step toward living a more intentional, purpose-driven life. Remember, purpose is not about perfection or having all the answers; it's about living in alignment with what matters most to you, day by day.

So, take a moment to reflect. What does purpose mean to you, and how might it already be influencing your life without you even realizing it? The answers may surprise you, and they may just be the beginning of a more meaningful journey.

Identifying Core Values and Beliefs

At the heart of discovering your purpose are your core values. These values are the fundamental beliefs that guide your actions, decisions, and behaviors. They serve as your internal compass, helping you navigate life's complexities and make choices that align with who you truly are. When you live in alignment with your values, life feels more meaningful and purposeful. When you stray from them, you often experience discomfort, dissatisfaction, or a sense of being lost.

Core values are deeply personal. They aren't dictated by society, your family, or your peers; rather, they are the principles you hold most dear, the things you believe in at your very core. For some, these values may include honesty, compassion, or creativity. For others, they may revolve around growth, freedom, or community. There is no right or wrong set of values—what matters is that they resonate with you and reflect your authentic self.

One of the most powerful aspects of identifying your core values is that it provides clarity in moments of uncertainty. When faced with tough decisions, you can turn to your values for guidance. For example, if one of your core values is integrity, you'll likely choose the path that feels honest and aligned with your ethical beliefs, even if it's not the easiest route. If another value is adventure, you might seek opportunities that push you out of your comfort zone and allow you to explore new horizons.

But how do you identify your core values? It often begins with reflection on your past experiences. Think about the moments in your life when you felt most fulfilled, proud, or at peace. What was happening during those times? What qualities were present in your actions or the environment around you? These positive experiences often point to your values being in alignment. On the other hand, consider times when you felt conflicted, unhappy, or disconnected. Chances are, one or more of your core values were being compromised.

Take a few moments to think about what values are most important to you. Here are a few questions to guide your reflection:

- What principles do I hold most dear?
- When have I felt most proud of myself? What values were present in that moment?
- What qualities do I admire most in others, and why?
- What values do I refuse to compromise, even when it's difficult?

By answering these questions, you'll start to notice recurring themes that point to your core values. Maybe you realize that you're driven by a desire for authenticity, always striving to show up as your true self in every situation. Or perhaps you discover that service to others is central to your life, guiding you to seek ways to make a difference in the world. Whatever your values may be, identifying them is a crucial step in discovering your purpose because they serve as the foundation upon which purpose is built.

Once you've identified your core values, it's important to reflect on how well your current life aligns with them. Are your decisions, relationships, and goals in harmony with your values?

If not, this misalignment may be a source of dissatisfaction or a signal that it's time to make changes. Living in alignment with your values allows you to live more authentically, which naturally leads to a deeper sense of purpose and fulfillment.

For example, if one of your core values is growth, but you feel stagnant in your career or personal life, this misalignment could cause frustration or restlessness. Recognizing this gives you the opportunity to pursue new challenges, seek education, or take risks that align more closely with your value of growth. Similarly, if you value connection but find yourself isolated or disconnected from meaningful relationships, this awareness can help you prioritize building stronger bonds with others.

Values not only help you understand what matters most to you—they also serve as a powerful tool for self-evaluation. When you face moments of doubt, confusion, or change, returning to your core values can offer clarity and direction. They remind you of who you are at your core and what you stand for, helping you stay grounded even in the midst of uncertainty.

As you move forward in this journey to discovering your purpose, remember that your values are the bedrock of everything you do. They shape your purpose, influence your decisions, and ultimately determine how fulfilled you feel in your life. By identifying and honoring your core values, you create a strong foundation upon which to build a life of meaning, passion, and purpose.

Take some time to sit with your values, reflect on them, and consider how they manifest in your life. Are you living in alignment with them? Are there areas where you need to recalibrate to ensure your values are guiding your path? The more you understand your values, the closer you will come to living a life that reflects your true purpose.

Exploring Personal Passions and Interests

If core values form the foundation of your purpose, then your passions are the fuel that propels it forward. Passions are the activities, topics, or causes that spark a sense of excitement and joy in your life. They are what make you feel alive, energized, and deeply connected to the moment. When your purpose aligns with your passions, you experience a powerful sense of fulfillment because you're doing something that matters to you on a deeply emotional level.

However, it's common for people to overlook or undervalue their passions, especially in the context of careers and responsibilities. Too often, passions are seen as hobbies or pastimes—something to indulge in only after the "real" work is done. But what if your passions could be more than just an escape? What if they could be central to discovering your purpose and shaping your personal and professional life?

To explore your passions is to dig deeper into what brings you joy and satisfaction. It's about recognizing the things that make time fly by because you're so immersed in the moment. When you're passionate about something, you naturally invest more energy and enthusiasm into it, and this investment often leads to mastery and fulfillment. That's why connecting your purpose with your passions is such a powerful combination.

So how do you begin to uncover your passions? Start by reflecting on what excites you the most. Here are some questions to guide your exploration:

- What activities or subjects make me lose track of time?
- What topics do I feel compelled to learn more about or discuss with others?
- When have I felt the most energized or alive, and what was I doing at that time?

- What hobbies, interests, or causes would I pursue if time and money were no obstacle?

These questions help you identify what drives you from within. Your passions are not always tied to what others expect of you or what seems "practical." They are deeply personal, often rooted in your own unique experiences, talents, and desires. By exploring them, you gain valuable insight into the kinds of activities or fields that resonate with your true self.

Some people may find that their passions are directly related to their professional lives. For example, if you're passionate about problem-solving and creativity, you might find fulfillment in fields like engineering, design, or entrepreneurship. Others may discover that their passions lie outside of their work and are more personal in nature—such as a love for art, music, or community service. While it's not always possible to turn every passion into a career, it is possible to integrate these passions into your life in meaningful ways.

One of the most important aspects of exploring your passions is allowing yourself the freedom to pursue them without judgment. Too often, we stifle our passions because we fear they aren't practical or socially acceptable. You may love painting, for example, but dismiss it because you think it's not a "serious" pursuit. But what if painting is the key to unlocking a deeper sense of creativity and expression that could ultimately enhance your life, your relationships, or even your career? Passions don't have to be profitable to be valuable. They enrich your life by feeding your soul.

As you explore your interests, you might also notice a pattern between your passions and your core values. For example, if you're passionate about environmental sustainability and one of your core values is responsibility, you might find that your purpose lies in advocating for environmental causes or living a more eco-friendly lifestyle. This intersection between what you love and what you believe in is a powerful indicator of your purpose.

It's also important to remember that passions evolve over time. What excites you today might not be the same as what energized you ten years ago, and that's okay. As you grow and experience new things, your interests will naturally shift and expand. The key is to remain open and curious, allowing yourself to continue discovering new passions along the way.

In some cases, exploring your passions might also lead you to reconsider your current path. If you're passionate about teaching but find yourself working in a field that doesn't involve education or mentorship, you might feel a sense of disconnect between your job and your true interests. Recognizing this misalignment is not a failure; it's an opportunity to reassess how you can incorporate more of what you love into your life. Whether it means pursuing a new career path, volunteering in a field you care about, or simply dedicating more time to your personal hobbies, aligning your life with your passions is an essential step toward living with purpose.

Passions, when embraced and nurtured, are powerful forces that bring energy and joy into your life. They connect you with your most authentic self, and they often lead to greater personal and professional fulfillment. So, take the time to explore what truly excites you, and don't be afraid to pursue it. Your passions are not distractions; they are guiding lights that point you toward a deeper sense of purpose and meaning.

Creating a Personal Mission Statement

Now that you've explored your values and passions, the next step in discovering your purpose is creating a personal mission statement. A mission statement is a concise declaration of who you are, what you stand for, and what you aim to accomplish in life. It serves as a guiding star, helping you stay focused on your purpose, especially during times of uncertainty or challenge. Think of it as a blueprint for how you want to live, outlining the principles and aspirations that matter most to you.

While the idea of crafting a personal mission statement may seem intimidating, it's a powerful tool for clarifying your purpose and aligning your life with what truly matters. The process of writing a mission statement forces you to distill your values, passions, and goals into a few key sentences, creating a clear picture of your purpose. Once it's written, your mission statement can serve as a daily reminder of the person you want to be and the life you want to lead.

The first step in creating a mission statement is reflecting on the key elements that shape your sense of purpose: your core values, your passions, and the impact you want to have on the world. Consider the following questions as you begin to draft your mission statement:

- What are the core values that guide my decisions and actions?
- What am I most passionate about, and how do these passions shape my life?
- What positive impact do I want to have on my family, community, or the world?
- How do I want to be remembered by those who know me?

These questions will help you focus on the most important aspects of your life and purpose. Your mission statement should be an authentic reflection of who you are, so there's no need to make it sound lofty or formal. The goal is to capture the essence of what drives you and what you hope to accomplish, in a way that resonates with you personally.

Let's look at an example. Suppose you've identified that your core values include compassion, personal growth, and community. You're passionate about mentoring others and helping people realize their potential. You want to have a lasting impact by inspiring others to lead more meaningful and fulfilling lives. A personal mission statement that reflects these values might look something like this:

"My mission is to inspire and support others in their journey of personal growth, to lead with compassion, and to create meaningful connections within my community. I strive to live a life of continuous learning and to make a positive impact through mentorship and kindness."

This statement is simple but powerful. It highlights the individual's values (compassion, growth, community), their passions (mentorship, inspiring others), and their purpose (to make a positive impact). A mission statement like this not only provides clarity on who you are, but it also serves as a reminder of the actions you can take each day to live in alignment with your purpose.

Another key aspect of a mission statement is its ability to guide decision-making. Life is filled with choices, and it's easy to become overwhelmed by competing priorities or external pressures. A well-crafted mission statement helps you stay grounded and focused on what truly matters. When faced with difficult decisions or life changes, you can turn to your mission statement as a reference point. Does this choice align with my values and purpose? Will it bring me closer to fulfilling my mission, or does it pull me away from it?

For example, if your mission is to live a life of creativity and adventure, but you find yourself in a job that stifles your creativity, your mission statement can serve as a catalyst for change. It reminds you of what's important and encourages you to make decisions that bring you closer to living your mission—whether that means pursuing new opportunities, taking creative risks, or making time for your passions outside of work.

As you create your own mission statement, don't feel pressured to get it perfect right away. Like your purpose, your mission statement will evolve over time as you grow and change. What's important is that it feels true to you in this moment and reflects the core principles and aspirations that guide your life.

Here are a few more tips for crafting your personal mission statement:

1. **Keep it Simple**: Your mission statement should be easy to remember and recite. Avoid overcomplicating it with too many details or buzzwords.
2. **Make it Authentic**: Don't write a mission statement based on what you think others expect of you. This is your statement, and it should reflect your unique values, passions, and goals.
3. **Focus on Impact**: Consider the positive impact you want to have on the world. A mission statement that connects your purpose to a greater good can be incredibly motivating.
4. **Be Open to Change**: As your life changes, so will your mission. Feel free to revisit and revise your mission statement over time to reflect your evolving purpose.

Creating a personal mission statement is not just about writing words on a page—it's about articulating your purpose and setting the intention to live by it every day. Once you've written your statement, make it visible. Put it on your desk, in your planner, or as the background on your phone. The more you remind yourself of your mission, the more likely you are to live in alignment with it.

Ultimately, your personal mission statement serves as a compass, guiding you toward a life that reflects your values, passions, and goals. It empowers you to make intentional choices and to pursue a purpose-driven life. So take the time to craft a mission statement that feels meaningful to you—it's an investment in your future, and in the fulfillment and purpose you seek.

Aligning Actions with Purpose

Having identified your core values, passions, and written your personal mission statement, the final step in this chapter is perhaps the most critical—aligning your actions with your purpose. It's one thing to have clarity on what matters most to you and what your mission is, but it's another thing entirely to ensure that your daily choices and behaviors reflect those guiding principles. Living with purpose requires consistent, intentional action.

Purpose is not a passive concept. It is dynamic and comes alive through the choices you make and the habits you build. You may have a clear sense of purpose, but without aligning your actions to that purpose, you risk feeling disconnected or unfulfilled. The key is ensuring that your actions, both big and small, are in harmony with your values and the life you want to create.

Consider this: every action you take either brings you closer to living your purpose or pulls you further away from it. Whether it's the career you pursue, the relationships you nurture, or how you spend your free time, each decision influences the alignment between who you are and how you live. When your actions are aligned with your purpose, life feels more satisfying, meaningful, and purposeful. When they aren't, you may feel out of sync, directionless, or dissatisfied.

The first step in aligning your actions with your purpose is to become more mindful of how you're currently spending your time and energy. Ask yourself:

- Are my daily actions moving me closer to fulfilling my mission?
- Am I spending time on activities or relationships that reflect my values?
- Do my habits support the life I want to live, or are they taking me off course?

One powerful exercise to help with this reflection is to evaluate how you're spending your time on a typical day or week. Write down your daily schedule, from the moment you wake up until you go to bed. Then, assess how much of that time is spent on activities that align with your purpose versus those that don't. You may find that much of your day is consumed by obligations or distractions that aren't truly meaningful to you. Recognizing this disconnect is the first step toward making more intentional choices.

For example, if one of your core values is personal growth but you're not dedicating any time to learning or self-improvement, this misalignment could lead to frustration. Similarly, if you value connection but find that your relationships feel shallow or transactional, you may need to invest more time and energy into deepening those connections. By being honest with yourself about how your actions align—or don't—with your purpose, you can start making adjustments.

Once you've identified areas where your actions are out of alignment, the next step is to create intentional habits that bring your life more in sync with your mission. Purposeful living isn't about making radical changes overnight. It's about small, consistent actions that reflect your values and move you toward your goals. These actions can be as simple as dedicating time each day to your passions, setting boundaries around how you spend your energy, or being more present in your relationships.

For example, if your mission involves helping others, you might choose to volunteer once a week or mentor someone in your field. If creativity is a core part of your purpose, you could commit to setting aside time each day to write, paint, or engage in a creative pursuit. Whatever your mission is, aligning your daily actions with that purpose helps you live more authentically and experience a deeper sense of fulfillment.

It's also important to remember that alignment doesn't mean perfection. Life is unpredictable, and there will be times when your actions don't perfectly reflect your purpose. You may take a job that doesn't fully align with your passions, or find yourself in a phase of life where your focus shifts due to external circumstances. That's okay. What matters is that you continue to revisit your mission and make adjustments as needed. Purpose is not a fixed destination—it's a continuous journey, and your actions are the vehicle that carries you along that path.

Another key to aligning your actions with your purpose is being willing to say no to things that don't serve you. This can be one of the hardest aspects of living with purpose because it requires you to prioritize what truly matters and let go of distractions, obligations, or relationships that are not in alignment. It's easy to get caught up in saying yes to everything—whether it's out of a desire to please others, meet societal expectations, or avoid discomfort. But saying yes to everything often means saying no to your own needs and values.

Living with purpose sometimes means making difficult choices, like leaving a job that doesn't align with your values, ending a relationship that no longer serves your growth, or setting boundaries that protect your time and energy. These decisions may not be easy, but they are necessary if you want to live a life that reflects your true purpose.

Finally, it's important to regularly reflect on your progress and celebrate your wins. Aligning your actions with your purpose is an ongoing process, and it's crucial to acknowledge the moments when you're living in alignment, even if they're small. These moments of alignment—when you're engaged in work that fulfills you, spending time with people who uplift you, or pursuing passions that ignite your soul—are what give life its richness and meaning.

As you continue on this journey, make time for regular check-ins with yourself. Ask whether your actions still align with your mission and whether any adjustments need to be made. By staying mindful of your purpose and continually aligning your actions with it, you'll create a life that feels deeply fulfilling and true to who you are.

In conclusion, living with purpose is not just about knowing your values or passions—it's about consistently making choices that reflect them. When your actions align with your purpose, you experience a sense of harmony and satisfaction that can't be achieved through external success alone. So, as you move forward, remember that purpose is lived out through the small, intentional choices you make every day. By aligning your actions with your mission, you will not only elevate your life but also inspire others to do the same.

{ **2** }

Chapter 2: Overcoming Limiting Beliefs

Understanding Limiting Beliefs
We all have stories we tell ourselves—narratives that shape how we view the world and our place within it. These stories often begin early in life, influenced by our families, teachers, friends, and the society we grow up in. Some of these stories are empowering, reminding us of our strengths and potential. But others, known as limiting beliefs, hold us back. They are the silent barriers that keep us from pursuing our dreams or embracing new opportunities. To overcome them, we first need to understand what limiting beliefs are, where they come from, and how they manifest in our daily lives.

A limiting belief is a thought or conviction that restricts you in some way. It's an internalized idea that convinces you that you can't do something, that you're not good enough, or that success, happiness, or fulfillment is beyond your reach. These beliefs are often subtle and operate below the surface of conscious thought, making them difficult to detect at first. Yet, they influence almost every decision you make, from the opportunities you pursue to how you view your capabilities.

Limiting beliefs typically form early in life. They might come from a critical comment made by a parent or teacher, an experience of failure that left a lasting impression, or societal messages about what is "possible" for someone of your background, gender, or education level. Over time, these beliefs become internalized, shaping how you see yourself and the world around you. They become part of the mental framework through which you make decisions, often without you even realizing it.

For example, imagine you were told as a child that you weren't creative. Perhaps a teacher dismissed your artwork or a parent discouraged your interest in writing or music. Over time, this single experience could evolve into a deep-seated belief that "I'm not creative," leading you to shy away from creative pursuits throughout your life. Similarly, if you grew up in a family where financial security was a constant struggle, you might develop the belief that "money is hard to come by," which could influence how you approach your career or manage your finances as an adult.

One of the most insidious aspects of limiting beliefs is that they often feel like objective truths. When you're under the influence of a limiting belief, it doesn't feel like you're being pessimistic or overly cautious. Instead, it feels like you're simply facing reality. Statements like "I'll never be successful," "I'm not smart enough to start my own business," or "I don't deserve happiness" seem, in the moment, like accurate reflections of who you are and what's possible for you.

But limiting beliefs are not truths. They are simply perceptions, often based on fear, past experiences, or societal conditioning. They create an invisible ceiling that keeps you from reaching your full potential. The good news is that, like all perceptions, limiting beliefs can be changed. Once you recognize them for what they are—mental constructs rather than immutable facts—you can begin to challenge and dismantle them.

Common limiting beliefs can take many forms. Here are a few examples:

- **"I'm not good enough."** This belief can manifest in a variety of areas, from relationships to career ambitions. It convinces you that, no matter how hard you try, you're destined to fall short.
- **"I don't have enough time."** Many people use this belief as a reason to avoid pursuing new opportunities or making changes. The truth is, we all have the same 24 hours in a day—it's how we choose to prioritize those hours that matters.
- **"I'll never succeed."** This belief can prevent you from even trying to achieve your goals, because it convinces you that failure is inevitable.
- **"I don't deserve happiness."** Rooted in feelings of unworthiness, this belief can sabotage your relationships, career, and overall well-being, as it stops you from seeking or accepting the joy you deserve.

The first step to overcoming limiting beliefs is awareness. You need to recognize these beliefs for what they are—mental obstacles that are holding you back. This can be difficult, as many limiting beliefs have been with you for so long that they feel like an ingrained part of your identity. However, by learning to identify the negative thoughts and patterns that arise in certain situations, you can begin to shine a light on the beliefs that are influencing your behavior.

Take a moment to reflect on areas in your life where you feel stuck or unfulfilled. Are there any repeating patterns of thought that come up when you think about these areas? For example, when you consider a new job opportunity, do you immediately think, "I'm not qualified for that"? When you think about your relationships, do you believe, "I'll never find love"? These thoughts are often clues that a limiting belief is at play.

It's important to remember that limiting beliefs are learned—they are not inherent to who you are. Just as they were formed, they can also be unlearned. By becoming aware of these beliefs, you've already taken the first step toward freeing yourself from their grip. In the next sections, we will explore how to identify your own limiting beliefs, challenge them, and replace them with empowering beliefs that support your growth and potential.

Understanding the nature of limiting beliefs is crucial to overcoming them. Once you recognize that these beliefs are not absolute truths, but rather perceptions influenced by your past, you open the door to new possibilities. By letting go of limiting beliefs, you make room for new opportunities, greater confidence, and a deeper sense of purpose in your life.

Identifying Your Own Limiting Beliefs

Now that you understand what limiting beliefs are and how they can shape your life, the next step is to uncover the specific limiting beliefs that are holding *you* back. This process requires self-reflection, honesty, and a willingness to explore the inner narratives that may be keeping you from reaching your full potential. Identifying your limiting beliefs is an essential part of the journey because it allows you to bring these unconscious thoughts into your awareness, where you can begin to challenge and change them.

Limiting beliefs often operate under the radar of your conscious mind. They influence your decisions, actions, and reactions in ways that can be subtle or deeply ingrained. You may not even realize they exist until you examine the patterns in your life that seem to repeat—whether it's always feeling stuck in a job you don't enjoy, struggling to maintain healthy relationships, or never quite reaching your goals. The limiting beliefs that underpin these patterns are the hidden obstacles preventing you from creating the life you want.

To begin identifying your own limiting beliefs, it's helpful to focus on areas of your life where you feel dissatisfied or unfulfilled. Think about the goals you've set for yourself but haven't achieved. Reflect on the dreams you've let go of, the fears that hold you back, or the feelings of inadequacy that arise when you're faced with new opportunities. These are often the places where limiting beliefs are at work.

Here are some questions to guide you in uncovering your own limiting beliefs:

1. **What is an area of your life where you feel stuck or blocked?**
   - Whether it's your career, relationships, health, or personal growth, identify one or more areas where you feel like you're not making progress or where you've hit a plateau. This is often where limiting beliefs are strongest.

2. **What do you tell yourself when you think about making a change or taking a risk in that area?**
   - Pay attention to the inner dialogue that arises when you contemplate doing something new or different. For example, if you're thinking about applying for

a promotion, do you automatically think, "I'm not qualified enough"? If you're considering starting a new business, does a voice in your head say, "I'll probably fail"? These thoughts provide clues to the limiting beliefs you hold.

3. **What stories do you tell yourself about your abilities and worth?**

    ◦ Everyone has an internal narrative about who they are, what they're capable of, and what they deserve. Listen to the stories you tell yourself. Are they empowering or disempowering? Do they build you up or hold you back? For example, if you consistently tell yourself, "I'm not good at public speaking," or "I'm not someone who can take risks," these are limiting beliefs that influence how you show up in the world.

4. **Where do you feel resistance when you try to take action?**

    ◦ Often, limiting beliefs reveal themselves through resistance. When you're trying to move forward toward a goal but keep finding reasons to procrastinate, hesitate, or avoid action, it's a sign that a limiting belief is in play. Ask yourself, "What am I afraid of?" and "What belief might be holding me back from taking this step?"

Another powerful exercise to help you identify limiting beliefs is journaling. Writing down your thoughts, feelings, and experiences can help you see patterns that you might otherwise miss. Set aside some time to write about a specific area of your life where you feel held back. What emotions come up? What are the recurring thoughts that arise? Do you notice any negative statements about yourself, your abilities, or your potential? These are often rooted in limiting beliefs.

For example, imagine you've always wanted to pursue a creative career, but you've never taken the leap. As you journal, you may uncover a recurring thought like, "I'm not talented enough to make it as an artist." This belief has likely been with you for years, influencing every decision you've made about your career. By recognizing this thought as a limiting belief rather than an objective truth, you can begin to challenge it.

It's also helpful to reflect on where these beliefs may have originated. Limiting beliefs often stem from childhood experiences, societal expectations, or negative feedback we've internalized over time. For instance, if you were repeatedly told as a child that financial success was only for people with a certain background or education, you might now carry the limiting belief that "people like me can't be wealthy." Recognizing the origin of a limiting belief can help you see it more clearly and detach from it.

As you uncover your limiting beliefs, it's important to approach this process with compassion rather than judgment. Remember, these beliefs were often formed as a way to protect you or make sense of the world, even if they're no longer serving you. Being hard on yourself for having limiting beliefs won't help you overcome them—instead, be curious and open to the possibility of change.

Once you've identified a limiting belief, you can begin to question its validity. Ask yourself:

- **Is this belief objectively true?**
  More often than not, you'll find that the answer is no. Just because you believe something doesn't mean it's a fact. For example, if your belief is "I'm not good enough to lead a

team," ask yourself whether there's any solid evidence to support that belief. Have you ever successfully led in any capacity before? Have you received positive feedback in leadership roles? Chances are, the belief is more a reflection of your fears than an objective truth.

- **Where did this belief come from?**
Understanding the origin of a limiting belief can help you recognize that it's not a fundamental truth about you—it's simply a belief you picked up along the way. Whether it came from a critical teacher, a negative experience, or societal expectations, knowing where the belief started can help you see it for what it is: a learned behavior that can be unlearned.

- **How has this belief affected my life?**
Reflect on the ways in which this belief has shaped your decisions, actions, and overall happiness. Has it held you back from pursuing your dreams? Has it kept you stuck in situations that don't serve you? Recognizing the impact of a limiting belief can give you the motivation to challenge and change it.

Identifying your limiting beliefs is a transformative process. By shining a light on the hidden thoughts that have been holding you back, you take the first step toward reclaiming your power and creating a life that reflects your true potential. The journey to overcoming these beliefs begins with awareness, and with that awareness comes the possibility of profound change.

Challenging and Reframing Limiting Beliefs

Now that you've identified your limiting beliefs, it's time to challenge them. This step is crucial because it allows you to break free from the mental barriers that have been holding you back.

Challenging a limiting belief involves questioning its validity, re-examining the evidence behind it, and ultimately reframing it into a belief that empowers rather than restricts you. It's about transforming those self-imposed limitations into possibilities and opening yourself up to new ways of thinking and being.

The process of challenging limiting beliefs starts with recognizing that these beliefs are not facts. They are simply interpretations—often flawed—of past experiences or societal conditioning. Just because you've believed something for a long time doesn't mean it's true. In fact, many of the beliefs that limit us are based on outdated information, misunderstandings, or fears that no longer serve us. Once you realize this, you can begin to dismantle the belief and replace it with something more constructive.

One of the most effective ways to challenge a limiting belief is to ask yourself a series of critical questions designed to test its validity. These questions force you to examine whether the belief is based on truth or assumption, and they help you see the belief from a new perspective. Let's break down this process step by step:

1. Is this belief true?

- This is the most fundamental question you can ask yourself when confronting a limiting belief. Often, we accept our beliefs as facts without ever questioning them. But when you pause and ask yourself, "Is this really true?" you open the door to new possibilities. For example, if your limiting belief is "I'm not good enough to lead a team," challenge it by asking if it's based on any real evidence. Have you ever failed as a leader? Or is it just something you assume about yourself without much proof? Most of the time, you'll find that your belief is not grounded in reality but in fear or insecurity.

2. What evidence do I have that supports this belief?

- After questioning whether the belief is true, it's important to examine the evidence—or lack thereof—that supports it. Take a closer look at your experiences. Has there ever been a time when this belief was proven wrong? For example, if you believe "I'm not creative," think back to moments when you've demonstrated creativity, even in small ways. Maybe you successfully solved a problem in a unique way or came up with an idea that was well-received by others. Often, you'll find that the evidence supporting your limiting belief is either nonexistent or greatly exaggerated.

3. What evidence contradicts this belief?

- Now, flip the script. Rather than focusing on why the belief might be true, start looking for reasons why it isn't. If your belief is "I always fail," think about times when you've succeeded. Even small wins count. Have you ever completed a difficult project, received positive feedback, or achieved a goal? Focusing on these moments helps dismantle the belief by proving that it isn't universally true. Every person has had successes, and acknowledging them allows you to see the belief for what it is—a distortion of reality.

4. How does holding onto this belief serve me?

- Believe it or not, we sometimes hold onto limiting beliefs because they serve a purpose, even if that purpose is negative. For example, holding onto the belief "I'll never succeed" might protect you from the fear of failure by keeping you from trying in the first place. In this way, the belief acts as a kind of psychological shield. But ask yourself: Is this shield really helping me, or is it holding me back? When you recognize that the belief is no longer serving you in a productive way, you can begin to let it go.

5. What would I do if I didn't have this belief?

- This is perhaps the most powerful question of all. Imagine for a moment that the limiting belief simply didn't exist. What would you be able to accomplish? How would your life be different? If the belief "I'm not good enough" were gone, what actions would you take toward your goals? This question forces you to visualize a life where you're not constrained by that belief, and it shows you that the possibilities for your life are far greater than you may have realized.

Once you've thoroughly challenged your limiting belief, the next step is to **reframe** it. Reframing is the process of replacing a limiting belief with a new, empowering belief that reflects your potential rather than your fears. The goal is to create a belief that encourages growth and helps you move toward the life you want. For example, let's say your limiting belief is "I'm not smart enough to start my own business." After challenging it, you might reframe it into something like, "I have the ability to learn and grow, and I'm capable of building a successful business."

Here are a few strategies to help you reframe your limiting beliefs:

1. Use affirmations to create new beliefs.

• Affirmations are positive, present-tense statements that reinforce your new belief. They help retrain your brain to focus on what's possible rather than on what's limiting. For example, if your limiting belief was "I'm not creative," you could replace it with the affirmation "I am a creative thinker, and I approach challenges with fresh ideas." By repeating this affirmation daily, you begin to shift your mindset from one of limitation to one of empowerment.

2. Focus on progress, not perfection.

• Reframing a limiting belief doesn't mean that you have to suddenly become perfect at everything. It's about focusing on growth and improvement. Instead of saying, "I have to be the best at this," try reframing it to "I'm committed to learning and improving every day." This takes the pressure off and allows you to see challenges as opportunities for growth, not as proof of failure.

3. Surround yourself with supportive people.

• The people you spend time with can have a big influence on your beliefs, so make sure you surround yourself with individuals who encourage your growth and challenge your limiting beliefs. If you're trying to reframe a belief about your career, for instance, spend time with people who have successfully achieved what you're striving for. Their positive energy and experiences can help reinforce your new beliefs.

4. Celebrate your wins.

- As you begin to challenge and reframe your limiting beliefs, it's important to celebrate your progress. Each time you take a step forward, no matter how small, acknowledge it. This reinforces the new belief and helps solidify it in your mind. Over time, these small victories will accumulate, and your new belief will become second nature.

Challenging and reframing limiting beliefs is not something that happens overnight, but with consistent effort, it can lead to profound change. By questioning the beliefs that have been holding you back, you open yourself up to a world of new possibilities. Instead of being governed by fear or past experiences, you begin to create your own reality—one that reflects your true potential and aligns with your goals. With each limiting belief you challenge, you take a step closer to living the life you truly deserve.

Rewriting Your Internal Narrative

Once you've challenged and reframed your limiting beliefs, it's time to take the next step: rewriting your internal narrative. The story you tell yourself about who you are, what you're capable of, and how the world works has a profound impact on every area of your life. This internal narrative is shaped by your beliefs, experiences, and perceptions, and it influences the decisions you make, the opportunities you pursue, and the way you handle challenges. If your internal story is rooted in limitation, fear, or self-doubt, it's time to rewrite it into one that reflects empowerment, growth, and possibility.

Your internal narrative is more than just a collection of thoughts; it's the lens through which you view the world. It affects how you interpret events, how you see yourself in relation to others, and how you respond to both success and failure. For example, someone with a limiting internal narrative might interpret a setback as confirmation of their inadequacy: "Of course, I failed. I'm not good enough." On the other hand, someone with an empowering internal narrative might see the same setback as a learning opportunity: "I didn't succeed this time, but I learned valuable lessons that will help me next time."

The goal of rewriting your internal narrative is to shift from a mindset of limitation to one of possibility. This doesn't mean ignoring challenges or pretending everything is perfect; rather, it means adopting a narrative that supports your growth, resilience, and ability to navigate difficulties in a constructive way. By consciously choosing to tell a different story about yourself, you can begin to create a new reality.

1. Recognize the Power of Your Story

The first step in rewriting your internal narrative is to recognize the power that your current story holds over your life. We all have a story that we've been telling ourselves for years—often without even realizing it. This story is shaped by our past experiences, the messages we've received from others, and the beliefs we've internalized along the way. For example, if you grew up hearing that you weren't good at math, you might have created a story around that belief: "I'm not good with numbers, so I'll never be able to handle my finances." Over time, this story becomes part of your identity, and you live your life based on that narrative.

But here's the thing: your story is not set in stone. You have the power to change it. The story you tell yourself can evolve as you grow and as your understanding of yourself deepens. Recognizing that your internal narrative is fluid, not fixed, gives you the freedom to rewrite it in a way that supports your goals and aspirations.

2. Examine the Current Story You're Telling Yourself

To begin rewriting your internal narrative, you need to first examine the story you're currently telling yourself. What is the dominant theme of your internal dialogue? Is it one of empowerment or limitation? Do you see yourself as someone who can overcome challenges and achieve your goals, or do you believe that success is out of reach for you?

Start by paying attention to the language you use when you talk to yourself, both in your thoughts and out loud. Do you often say things like, "I can't," "I'm not good enough," or "This always happens to me"? These phrases are clues to the limiting story you've been telling yourself. Write down some of these recurring thoughts and examine them closely. What beliefs are behind these statements? How do they make you feel? What actions do they lead to (or prevent you from taking)?

For example, if your internal narrative includes the belief "I always fail," how has that affected your actions? Perhaps you've stopped trying to pursue certain goals because you've already decided that failure is inevitable. Or maybe you approach new opportunities with hesitation and self-doubt, which in turn leads to outcomes that reinforce your limiting belief.

3. Rewrite the Story in a Way That Empowers You

Once you've identified the current story you're telling yourself, the next step is to rewrite it in a way that empowers you. This involves shifting the narrative from one of limitation to one of possibility. Instead of focusing on what you can't do or haven't achieved, start telling a story that emphasizes your strengths, your potential, and your ability to grow.

For example, if your current narrative is "I'm not smart enough to succeed in my career," you can reframe it as "I have the ability to learn, grow, and improve, and I'm committed to doing whatever it takes to achieve my goals." Notice how this new story is focused on growth and effort rather than on a fixed sense of ability. It's not about denying challenges or pretending that everything will come easily; it's about recognizing that you have the power to learn and improve over time.

Here are some strategies to help you rewrite your internal narrative:

- **Focus on progress, not perfection.**
  Instead of telling yourself that you need to be perfect in order to succeed, focus on the progress you're making. Acknowledge the steps you've taken, the skills you've developed, and the lessons you've learned along the way. This shifts the narrative from one of inadequacy to one of continual growth.
- **Emphasize your strengths and achievements.**
  It's easy to get caught up in what you haven't done or what you think you lack. But take a moment to reflect on your strengths, talents, and accomplishments. What have you done well? What are you proud of? By incorporating these strengths into your new narrative, you remind yourself that you are capable of achieving great things.
- **Use positive, empowering language.**
  The words you use in your internal dialogue matter. Instead of saying, "I'll never be able to do this," try saying, "I'm working on this, and I'm getting better every day." Positive language reinforces an empowering narrative and helps rewire your brain to focus on possibilities rather than limitations.

4. Practice Your New Story Daily

Rewriting your internal narrative is not a one-time event—it's a daily practice. Just as it took time for your limiting beliefs to become ingrained, it will take time to fully embrace your new, empowering narrative. But with consistent effort, you can begin to shift the way you see yourself and the world.

One effective way to practice your new story is through daily affirmations. These are positive statements that reflect your new beliefs and reinforce your empowering narrative. For example, if you've rewritten your story to emphasize your ability to grow and succeed, your affirmation might be something like, "I am capable of achieving my goals, and I trust in my ability to learn and grow." Repeat this affirmation to yourself every day, especially when you encounter challenges or setbacks.

In addition to affirmations, visualization can be a powerful tool for reinforcing your new narrative. Take a few minutes each day to visualize yourself living out your new story. Imagine yourself confidently pursuing your goals, overcoming obstacles, and achieving success. The more vividly you can picture yourself embodying your new narrative, the more real it will begin to feel.

5. Surround Yourself with Supportive Influences

As you work to rewrite your internal narrative, it's important to surround yourself with people and influences that reinforce your new story. Seek out individuals who believe in your potential and encourage your growth. Whether it's friends, mentors, or role models, being around positive, supportive people can help you stay committed to your new narrative.

It's also helpful to consume media—books, podcasts, videos—that align with your new beliefs. The more you immerse yourself in empowering content, the more your internal narrative will shift toward one of possibility and success.

By rewriting your internal narrative, you take control of the story you tell yourself about who you are and what you're capable of. This new story becomes the foundation for your actions, decisions, and achievements. Instead of being limited by old beliefs, you create a narrative that empowers you to reach your highest potential. And as you live out this new story, you'll find that the life you once dreamed of is not only possible but within your grasp.

Embracing a Growth Mindset

As you rewrite your internal narrative and challenge your limiting beliefs, one of the most powerful tools you can adopt is a **growth mindset**. Coined by psychologist Carol Dweck, a growth mindset is the belief that your abilities and intelligence can be developed through effort, learning, and perseverance. It's the opposite of a fixed mindset, which assumes that your talents and capabilities are static and unchangeable. When you embrace a growth mindset, you begin to see challenges as opportunities for development rather than as roadblocks, and you view failure as a stepping stone to success.

Adopting a growth mindset is key to overcoming limiting beliefs because it shifts your focus from "what I am" to "what I can become." It encourages you to move beyond your current limitations and to focus on continuous improvement. This mindset not only helps you achieve more, but it also reduces the fear of failure, making it easier to take risks and embrace new experiences.

1. Seeing Challenges as Opportunities for Growth

In a fixed mindset, challenges are something to avoid. If you believe that your abilities are set in stone, facing a difficult task can feel like a threat to your sense of competence. You might think, "If I fail at this, it proves I'm not good enough." But when you adopt a growth mindset, challenges take on a completely different meaning. Instead of being something to fear, they become valuable opportunities to stretch your abilities and learn new skills.

For example, if you've always believed that you're bad at public speaking, a fixed mindset would tell you to avoid situations where you have to speak in front of others. But with a growth mindset, you would see public speaking as a skill you can develop. Instead of focusing on your fear of failure, you would look at each speaking opportunity as a chance to improve. With each experience, you would become more confident, more skilled, and better able to handle the challenges that once seemed daunting.

Adopting a growth mindset helps you reframe challenges from threats into opportunities. It allows you to approach difficult situations with curiosity and a willingness to learn, knowing that even if you don't succeed right away, you'll gain valuable experience that will help you grow.

2. Learning from Failure

A key component of a growth mindset is the ability to learn from failure. In a fixed mindset, failure is seen as evidence of your limitations. If you fail, it must mean you're not smart enough, talented enough, or capable enough to succeed. This mindset can keep you from taking risks or trying new things because the fear of failure is too great.

But in a growth mindset, failure is viewed as an essential part of the learning process. It's not something to be ashamed of or to avoid—it's a natural and necessary step on the path to success. Instead of seeing failure as a reflection of your inadequacy, you begin to see it as an opportunity to gain insight, adjust your approach, and come back stronger.

For example, if you start a new business and it doesn't succeed right away, a fixed mindset might lead you to think, "I'm just not cut out for this." But a growth mindset would allow you to view the experience differently: "What can I learn from this? How can I improve my strategy next time?" This mindset keeps you moving forward, even in the face of setbacks, and it helps you turn every failure into a learning opportunity.

3. The Power of "Yet"

One of the simplest but most powerful tools for cultivating a growth mindset is the word **"yet."** This small word has the ability to completely change the way you view your abilities and your progress. When you say, "I can't do this," you're accepting defeat and reinforcing a fixed mindset. But when you add the word "yet"—"I can't do this yet"—you open up the possibility for growth.

The word "yet" reminds you that your abilities are not fixed. Just because you haven't mastered something today doesn't mean you won't be able to in the future. It reinforces the idea that learning and improvement are ongoing processes. By adding "yet" to your internal dialogue, you shift from a mindset of limitation to one of potential.

For example, if you're learning a new language and struggling to communicate fluently, a fixed mindset might lead you to say, "I'm just not good at languages." But with a growth mindset, you would say, "I'm not fluent yet." This simple shift in language reminds you that mastery is a process, and with continued effort, you will improve.

4. Focusing on Effort Over Results

In a fixed mindset, success is often measured solely by outcomes. If you don't achieve the desired result, it's easy to feel like a failure. But in a growth mindset, the focus shifts from outcomes to effort. Instead of only valuing the end result, you begin to value the process of learning, growing, and improving along the way.

Focusing on effort allows you to appreciate your progress, even when you haven't yet reached your ultimate goal. It also helps you develop resilience, as you come to understand that setbacks and challenges are just part of the journey. With a growth mindset, you learn to celebrate your efforts, knowing that each step forward—no matter how small—brings you closer to success.

For example, let's say you're working on a fitness goal, and after a few months, you haven't yet achieved the physical transformation you hoped for. In a fixed mindset, you might feel discouraged and give up. But with a growth mindset, you would recognize the effort you've put in, the strength you've gained, and the habits you've built. By focusing on effort rather than the final result, you stay motivated to keep going, knowing that continued effort will lead to progress over time.

5. Cultivating Resilience and Persistence

One of the greatest benefits of a growth mindset is that it fosters resilience and persistence. When you believe that your abilities can be developed, you're more likely to persevere through difficulties and setbacks. Instead of giving up at the first sign of failure, you keep pushing forward, knowing that each challenge is an opportunity to grow stronger.

Resilience is essential for long-term success, whether in your personal or professional life. Challenges are inevitable, but with a growth mindset, you develop the mental and emotional tools to navigate them. You learn to see setbacks not as dead-ends, but as detours on the road to success. This mindset allows you to bounce back from adversity and continue striving toward your goals, even when the journey gets tough.

For example, if you're pursuing a career goal and encounter obstacles along the way—such as rejections, missed opportunities, or slow progress—a fixed mindset might lead you to give up. But with a growth mindset, you would see these challenges as temporary. You would recognize that success is a process that requires persistence, and you would continue working toward your goal with renewed determination.

In the end, embracing a growth mindset is about understanding that your potential is not fixed. It's about recognizing that with effort, learning, and persistence, you can grow into the person you want to be. By cultivating this mindset, you empower yourself to move beyond your current limitations and to reach new heights of personal and professional growth.

As you continue your journey of overcoming limiting beliefs, remember that the story you tell yourself is constantly evolving. By adopting a growth mindset, you ensure that your story is one of possibility, resilience, and continual improvement. You are not defined by your past, your current challenges, or your perceived limitations—you are defined by your ability to grow, learn, and become the best version of yourself.

{ **3** }

Chapter 3: Building Resilience

Understanding Resilience and Its Importance
Resilience is the ability to adapt and bounce back when things don't go as planned. It's the mental toughness that allows you to weather life's inevitable storms, emerge stronger, and keep moving forward. But resilience is more than just endurance; it's about actively learning from challenges, processing adversity, and using those experiences as fuel for growth. In a world full of uncertainties, building resilience is not just helpful—it's essential.

At its core, resilience is the ability to recover from setbacks and remain motivated in the face of difficulty. It's what allows some people to keep going after losing a job, facing rejection, or experiencing failure. While many might see adversity as a barrier, resilient individuals see it as an opportunity to develop their skills, strengthen their character, and refine their approach. This doesn't mean they don't feel the pain or stress of hardship. Instead, they've developed the emotional tools to process these feelings and use them as stepping stones.

The importance of resilience cannot be overstated, especially when it comes to personal and professional growth. In your personal life, resilience enables you to maintain strong relationships, overcome loss, and handle changes that might otherwise be overwhelming. It helps you remain calm in the face of challenges and

{ 43 }

find solutions to problems rather than giving in to frustration. Professionally, resilience allows you to cope with pressure, manage stress, and remain effective under difficult circumstances. It ensures that setbacks don't define your progress, and that failure is viewed as part of the journey, not the end of the road.

Imagine two individuals working toward a common goal. One faces setbacks and immediately gives up, thinking that the obstacles are a sign that they're not cut out for the task. The other person, facing the same challenges, views the situation differently. They take time to reflect on what went wrong, adjust their approach, and try again with renewed determination. It's not just the initial talent or intelligence that sets these two people apart—it's resilience.

Resilience isn't a trait you're born with. While some may have a natural tendency to handle adversity better than others, resilience is a skill that anyone can cultivate. It's about shifting your mindset, developing emotional awareness, and creating a framework that allows you to process challenges productively. The good news is that resilience can grow over time with intentional practice, and it's a skill that benefits all aspects of your life.

The journey to building resilience begins with understanding its value and realizing that setbacks and challenges are not just obstacles—they are opportunities. Whether you're facing a personal loss, dealing with professional failure, or navigating the complexities of everyday life, resilience is what will carry you through. Instead of fearing adversity, resilient people embrace it, knowing that on the other side of hardship lies growth.

This doesn't mean that resilience is about ignoring difficulties or suppressing emotions. It's quite the opposite. Resilient individuals are often very in tune with their emotions. They allow themselves to feel the discomfort, frustration, or sadness that comes with failure, but they don't let these emotions control their actions. Instead, they process these emotions constructively, which allows them to gain valuable insights and make better decisions moving forward.

Building resilience also means being proactive about your growth. It's not just about surviving tough times; it's about thriving in spite of them. This means actively seeking out challenges, stretching your comfort zone, and continuously working to improve yourself. The more you challenge yourself, the more opportunities you have to build resilience, as each experience teaches you how to cope, adapt, and grow.

Ultimately, resilience is a combination of emotional strength, mental flexibility, and a proactive approach to life's challenges. By understanding its importance and consciously working to cultivate it, you can navigate setbacks with greater ease and emerge from adversity stronger than before. In the following sections, we'll dive deeper into practical ways to build this skill and how to apply it to both your personal and professional life, but the foundation remains the same: resilience is the key to not just surviving, but thriving.

Cultivating a Positive Mindset

A positive mindset is the cornerstone of resilience. It's what helps you stay focused on possibilities rather than problems, solutions rather than setbacks, and growth rather than defeat. Cultivating a positive mindset doesn't mean ignoring life's challenges or pretending everything is perfect. Rather, it's about approaching adversity with optimism and a belief in your ability to overcome it. It's the belief that, no matter how difficult the situation may seem, there is always a way forward.

At the heart of this mindset is the power of optimism. Optimism is not blind faith, but a conscious choice to focus on the good, even when things go wrong. It's about believing that your efforts will make a difference and that challenges are temporary, not permanent. When you adopt an optimistic perspective, you're more likely to see setbacks as opportunities to learn and grow, rather than as insurmountable obstacles.

For example, imagine you've applied for a promotion at work, but you didn't get the job. A pessimistic mindset might lead you to think, "I'll never be good enough," or "I should just stop trying." But with a positive mindset, you would look at the situation differently. You might think, "This is a chance for me to improve my skills," or "There will be more opportunities in the future, and I'll be ready for them." This shift in thinking doesn't change the outcome, but it changes your ability to move forward in a constructive way.

Another key component of a positive mindset is the practice of **gratitude**. Gratitude is the habit of focusing on what you have rather than what you lack. When faced with challenges, it's easy to fixate on what's going wrong and to lose sight of the good things in your life. Practicing gratitude helps you maintain perspective and reminds you that, even in difficult times, there is still much to be thankful for. Gratitude doesn't eliminate challenges, but it changes the way you perceive them, making them feel less overwhelming.

Gratitude can be cultivated in small ways. It could be as simple as taking a few minutes each day to write down three things you're grateful for. This practice trains your brain to look for the positives, even on tough days. Over time, it rewires your thinking, making it easier to maintain a positive outlook, even when faced with adversity.

One of the most powerful tools in cultivating a positive mindset is **reframing**. Reframing is the practice of looking at a situation from a different perspective. It's about finding a new angle, a silver lining, or a lesson within the challenge. For instance, if you lose a big client in your business, your initial reaction might be one of disappointment or frustration. However, reframing allows you to ask, "What can I learn from this?" or "How can I use this experience to improve my approach in the future?" Reframing turns challenges into learning experiences, helping you grow from the situation rather than being defeated by it.

Reframing can be applied in nearly every aspect of life. Whether you're facing personal challenges, professional setbacks, or emotional struggles, taking a moment to shift your perspective can make a world of difference. Instead of asking, "Why is this happening to me?" you can ask, "What is this teaching me?" or "How can I use this experience to become stronger?"

One of the biggest obstacles to maintaining a positive mindset is **negative self-talk**. We all have an internal dialogue, and often, it can be our harshest critic. When things don't go as planned, that voice might say, "You're not good enough," or "You always fail." This type of thinking is damaging to your resilience because it reinforces a fixed mindset—one that believes you are stuck in your current state and incapable of improvement.

To cultivate a positive mindset, it's crucial to challenge and replace negative self-talk with positive affirmations. When that critical voice speaks up, question it. Is it really true that you always fail? Or is this one setback in a long journey of successes and challenges? By reframing these thoughts and replacing them with affirmations like, "I'm learning and growing every day," or "I have the ability to improve and succeed," you start to shift your mindset from one of limitation to one of possibility.

Over time, cultivating a positive mindset becomes second nature. It doesn't mean you won't feel disappointment, frustration, or doubt—those are natural emotions that everyone experiences. But it does mean that you'll be able to move through those emotions more quickly, with the knowledge that you have the power to grow and adapt. A positive mindset gives you the mental flexibility to handle life's ups and downs with grace and determination.

In summary, cultivating a positive mindset is about choosing optimism, practicing gratitude, reframing challenges, and replacing negative self-talk with empowering affirmations. It's the foundation of resilience, allowing you to approach life's difficulties with confidence and a belief in your ability to overcome them. By developing this mindset, you'll be better equipped to face challenges head-on, turn setbacks into opportunities, and continue growing toward your goals.

Learning from Setbacks and Failures

Setbacks and failures are an inevitable part of life. No matter how well you plan or how hard you work, there will be times when things don't go as expected. But what sets resilient people apart is how they respond to these challenges. Rather than viewing failure as an endpoint, they see it as a stepping stone—a chance to learn, grow, and improve. Learning from setbacks is a crucial part of building resilience, and it begins with shifting your perspective on failure.

In our culture, failure often carries a negative connotation. Many of us are conditioned to avoid it at all costs, seeing it as a reflection of our inadequacy or lack of ability. But the truth is, failure is one of the most powerful teachers. Some of the most successful people in the world have experienced failure—often multiple times. What sets them apart is that they didn't allow their failures to define them. Instead, they used these experiences as opportunities to learn and improve.

When you face a setback, the first step is to **reframe** it. Instead of asking, "Why did this happen to me?" ask, "What can I learn from this?" This shift in thinking allows you to approach the situation with curiosity rather than frustration. Every failure, no matter how painful, contains valuable lessons if you're willing to look for them. By analyzing what went wrong, you can gain insight into your own behavior, decision-making, and strategies. This information can then be used to adjust your approach moving forward, making you more likely to succeed in the future.

Take, for example, someone who starts a new business venture that ultimately fails. At first glance, it might seem like a waste of time and effort. But upon reflection, they might realize that they didn't do enough market research or that they underestimated the amount of capital they needed to get started. These are invaluable lessons that can be applied to future endeavors. Without experiencing that initial failure, they might never have gained this insight.

Embracing a growth mindset is key to learning from setbacks. A growth mindset, as opposed to a fixed mindset, is the belief that abilities and intelligence can be developed through effort and learning. People with a growth mindset see failure as a natural part of the learning process. They understand that no one is perfect and that mistakes are opportunities to improve. In contrast, those with a fixed mindset believe that their abilities are static, and failure is a reflection of their inherent limitations. This belief often leads to avoiding challenges altogether, as failure becomes something to be feared rather than embraced.

When you adopt a growth mindset, failure no longer feels like a personal attack. Instead, it becomes a tool for improvement. The key is to approach setbacks with **resilience and adaptability**. Rather than giving up when things don't go your way, you take the time to reflect on what happened and find ways to adjust. This might mean developing new skills, changing your approach, or seeking advice from others who have been through similar experiences. The important thing is that you keep moving forward, no matter how many times you fall.

One effective way to learn from setbacks is to **conduct a personal review** after each failure. This doesn't have to be an extensive process, but it's important to reflect on what went wrong, why it happened, and what you can do differently next time. Ask yourself questions like:

- What factors contributed to this setback?
- What actions could I have taken to avoid this outcome?
- What have I learned about myself through this experience?
- How can I apply these lessons moving forward?

This process of reflection turns failure into a powerful learning tool. Rather than feeling defeated, you come away with actionable insights that make you more resilient and better equipped for future challenges.

Another important aspect of learning from failure is developing **emotional resilience**. Setbacks often come with a range of emotions—disappointment, frustration, and even self-doubt. It's natural to feel these things, but the key is not to let them overwhelm you. Resilient people acknowledge their emotions but don't allow them to dictate their actions. Instead, they process these feelings in a healthy way, using them as motivation to keep going.

One way to develop emotional resilience is to **practice self-compassion**. When you experience failure, it's easy to be harsh on yourself, blaming yourself for not being good enough or not trying hard enough. But self-criticism only deepens the emotional wounds caused by failure. Instead, treat yourself with the same kindness and understanding you would offer a friend going through a difficult time. Remind yourself that failure is a part of life and that everyone, no matter how successful, has experienced it at some point.

Self-compassion allows you to move through the emotional pain of setbacks without getting stuck in self-blame or defeat. It gives you the emotional space to reflect, learn, and grow from the experience.

Ultimately, learning from setbacks and failures is about adopting a mindset that views challenges as opportunities for growth. It's about seeing failure not as the end of the road, but as a valuable part of the journey. By reframing your approach to setbacks, embracing a growth mindset, and practicing emotional resilience, you'll become stronger, wiser, and more capable of achieving your goals. Resilience isn't about avoiding failure—it's about using it as fuel for your future success.

Developing Emotional Agility

Emotional agility is the ability to navigate your emotions in a flexible, adaptive way without letting them control your actions or decisions. It's not about avoiding negative emotions, but rather learning how to process and respond to them in a healthy and constructive manner. Emotional agility is a critical component of resilience because, when faced with challenges, your emotional response can either propel you forward or hold you back.

Life is full of unexpected twists, and your emotional state can fluctuate based on external events. A difficult conversation at work, a personal loss, or a failure in your business can all trigger strong emotional reactions like anger, sadness, or frustration. While it's natural to feel these emotions, it's how you respond to them that determines your level of resilience. Emotional agility allows you to acknowledge these feelings without being overwhelmed by them, enabling you to continue moving forward despite emotional turbulence.

The first step in developing emotional agility is **recognizing and accepting your emotions**. This may seem straightforward, but many people struggle to fully acknowledge their feelings, especially when those emotions are uncomfortable. We live in a culture that often promotes "positive thinking" at the expense of authentic emotional experiences. While it's important to maintain optimism, it's equally essential to allow yourself to feel a full range of emotions, including the difficult ones.

When faced with adversity, take a moment to pause and identify what you're feeling. Are you angry because you were passed over for a promotion? Are you disappointed that a project didn't turn out as expected? Whatever the emotion, give it a name. Simply labeling your feelings—whether it's frustration, sadness, or anxiety—helps you gain clarity and detachment. This act of naming your emotions creates a gap between you and the feeling, allowing you to view it more objectively.

Emotional agility doesn't mean suppressing or ignoring your feelings. It's about **acknowledging them without letting them dictate your behavior**. After identifying what you're feeling, ask yourself how you want to respond. Do you want to lash out in anger, or would you rather take a step back and approach the situation calmly? This moment of reflection is crucial in developing emotional resilience. It allows you to choose a response that aligns with your values and long-term goals, rather than reacting impulsively in the heat of the moment.

Consider a scenario where you've received negative feedback at work. Your initial emotional reaction might be defensiveness or hurt, leading you to dismiss the feedback or become combative. But with emotional agility, you can take a step back, recognize your feelings, and ask yourself how best to respond. You might decide that, instead of reacting defensively, you'll reflect on the feedback, learn from it, and use it as an opportunity for growth. This approach not only helps you build resilience but also strengthens your ability to handle criticism constructively.

A key element of emotional agility is the ability to **shift your perspective**. When you're in the midst of strong emotions, it's easy to get caught in a narrow view of the situation. You might feel like the problem you're facing is insurmountable or that the feelings you're experiencing will last forever. But emotional agility encourages you to take a broader, more balanced perspective. It's about reminding yourself that emotions are temporary and that no situation is as permanent or all-encompassing as it may feel in the moment.

One technique for shifting your perspective is to ask yourself, "Will this matter in a week? A month? A year?" This question helps you put the situation into context and realize that, while it might feel overwhelming right now, its impact will likely diminish over time. This shift in perspective allows you to approach the situation with greater calm and rationality, rather than being swept away by your immediate emotional response.

Self-awareness plays a vital role in emotional agility. Being aware of your emotional triggers—situations that cause you to react strongly—can help you prepare for and manage those reactions more effectively. For instance, if you know that receiving criticism tends to make you defensive, you can practice pausing and taking a deep breath before responding when faced with negative feedback. By becoming more self-aware, you give yourself the space to choose how to respond, rather than letting your emotions take control.

Another essential aspect of emotional agility is **self-compassion**. When you're going through a tough time, it's easy to fall into the trap of self-criticism, blaming yourself for the situation or for how you're feeling. But self-compassion involves treating yourself with the same kindness and understanding you would offer to a friend in a similar situation. Instead of berating yourself for feeling sad or frustrated, acknowledge that it's okay to feel this way and that it's a normal part of being human.

Research has shown that self-compassion helps people recover more quickly from setbacks and reduces the emotional toll of failure. When you approach yourself with kindness, you're more likely to bounce back from adversity with a clearer mind and greater emotional resilience. Self-compassion isn't about letting yourself off the hook, but rather about recognizing your humanity and allowing yourself the grace to learn and grow from your experiences.

In conclusion, developing emotional agility is a crucial skill for building resilience. By learning to recognize and accept your emotions, shifting your perspective, practicing self-awareness, and cultivating self-compassion, you can navigate life's challenges with greater flexibility and strength. Emotional agility doesn't mean avoiding negative emotions; it means embracing them as part of your journey and using them to fuel your personal and professional growth. Through this practice, you'll be better equipped to face setbacks and keep moving forward, no matter what obstacles arise.

Cultivating Optimism and a Positive Outlook

Resilience is not just about enduring hardships—it's also about maintaining a sense of optimism and a positive outlook in the face of adversity. Cultivating optimism doesn't mean ignoring difficulties or pretending everything is fine when it's not. Instead, it's about developing a mindset that focuses on possibilities, solutions, and the belief that setbacks are temporary and manageable. A positive outlook empowers you to stay motivated, find opportunities in challenges, and keep moving forward when things get tough.

Optimism is a powerful tool because it shapes how you perceive and respond to difficulties. When you have an optimistic mindset, you're more likely to view challenges as opportunities for growth rather than insurmountable obstacles. This doesn't mean denying reality or refusing to acknowledge problems, but it means choosing to focus on what can be done rather than what has gone wrong. Optimists see setbacks as temporary and specific to certain situations, rather than as personal failures or indicators of broader problems in their lives.

One way to cultivate optimism is by **reframing negative experiences**. When something doesn't go as planned, it's easy to dwell on the negatives and let frustration or disappointment take over. But an optimistic mindset challenges you to look at the same situation from a different angle. Instead of asking, "Why is this happening to me?" try asking, "What can I learn from this?" or "How can I grow through this experience?" Reframing negative situations helps you shift from a mindset of helplessness to one of empowerment and possibility.

Take, for example, a person who loses their job unexpectedly. An initial reaction might be panic, fear, or self-doubt. But someone who practices optimism would look beyond the immediate setback and ask themselves, "What new opportunities might this open up for me? Is there something else I've always wanted to pursue?" This shift in thinking not only reduces the emotional toll of the situation but also opens up new possibilities for the future.

Another key to developing a positive outlook is **practicing gratitude**. Research has shown that gratitude has a powerful impact on mental health and well-being. When you focus on what you're grateful for, it becomes easier to maintain a positive perspective, even during difficult times. Gratitude helps you shift your attention away from what's lacking or going wrong and instead appreciate the good things in your life, no matter how small. It's a way of reminding yourself that, even in challenging moments, there are still reasons to feel hopeful and optimistic.

One effective way to incorporate gratitude into your daily life is by keeping a **gratitude journal**. Each day, write down three things you're grateful for. These don't have to be big, life-changing events; they can be as simple as a kind word from a friend, a sunny day, or a small achievement. The practice of writing down your gratitude helps train your mind to notice and appreciate the positives, making it easier to maintain an optimistic outlook over time.

Optimism also involves **believing in your own ability to overcome challenges**. Resilient people have a sense of self-efficacy—the belief that they have the skills and resources to handle whatever comes their way. This doesn't mean they believe they'll never face difficulties, but they trust their ability to navigate them when they arise. Building this belief in yourself is crucial for cultivating optimism because it gives you the confidence to face challenges with a solution-oriented mindset.

To strengthen your sense of self-efficacy, reflect on times in the past when you successfully overcame obstacles. Remind yourself of the skills, strengths, and strategies you used to get through those tough times. This reflection not only boosts your confidence but also serves as a reminder that you have a track record of re-silience. When you trust in your ability to overcome challenges, it becomes easier to approach new setbacks with optimism and de-termination.

In addition to reframing negative experiences, practicing grat-itude, and building self-efficacy, another important element of optimism is **visualizing positive outcomes**. Visualization is a pow-erful tool that helps you mentally rehearse success before it hap-pens. When you visualize yourself overcoming a challenge or achieving a goal, your brain creates a mental blueprint of success. This not only boosts your motivation but also primes your mind to focus on actions that will lead to positive results.

For instance, if you're facing a difficult project at work, take a few minutes to close your eyes and imagine yourself successfully completing it. Picture the steps you'll take, the obstacles you'll overcome, and how you'll feel once it's finished. This mental re-hearsal not only builds your confidence but also helps you stay focused on the end goal, even when the process becomes challeng-ing.

It's also important to **surround yourself with positivity**. The people you spend time with can have a significant impact on your mindset and outlook. If you're constantly around negativ-ity—whether it's from friends, family, or colleagues—it can be dif-ficult to maintain an optimistic perspective. On the other hand, being around positive, supportive people who believe in you and encourage your growth can help you stay motivated and focused on the possibilities ahead.

Consider building a network of people who uplift you, whether it's through professional mentorship, friendships, or communities that share your values. These relationships serve as a source of en-couragement and inspiration, helping you stay positive and resilient when faced with challenges. In turn, you can also become a source of positivity for others, creating a cycle of support and optimism that benefits everyone involved.

Ultimately, cultivating optimism is about choosing to focus on possibilities, solutions, and growth. It's about believing that, no matter what challenges come your way, there is always a way forward. By reframing negative experiences, practicing gratitude, building self-efficacy, visualizing positive outcomes, and surrounding yourself with positivity, you can develop a mindset that not only helps you endure setbacks but also empowers you to thrive through them.

A positive outlook isn't about denying reality or avoiding difficulties—it's about approaching life with hope, confidence, and a belief that you have the power to shape your future. Through this lens of optimism, resilience becomes more than just enduring hardships—it becomes the ability to find strength, opportunity, and growth in every experience.

{ 4 }

Chapter 4: Creating Positive Habits

The Science of Habit Formation

Understanding how habits are formed is the first step to intentionally creating positive changes in your life. At its core, habit formation is rooted in the brain's ability to create neural pathways that automate actions. This process makes repeated behaviors easier and more efficient over time. When we break down the science of habit formation, we find a simple cycle known as the habit loop: **cue, routine, and reward**. This loop explains why habits form and, more importantly, how we can use it to create lasting positive habits.

The **cue** is the trigger that initiates the habit. It can be anything—a time of day, a location, an emotional state, or even another habit. For example, the sound of your alarm clock in the morning serves as a cue to start your daily routine. Without the cue, the habit doesn't start, which is why identifying the cues that trigger both positive and negative behaviors is key to understanding your habits.

Next comes the **routine**, which is the actual behavior you engage in when the cue occurs. This is the action or series of actions that has become ingrained in your day-to-day life. It could be something simple, like brushing your teeth after breakfast, or something more complex, like your entire morning exercise routine. The routine is where habits truly take shape, and it's the part that becomes automatic over time through repetition.

Finally, there's the **reward**, the part of the cycle that reinforces the habit. Every habit, no matter how trivial, provides some kind of reward. Sometimes the reward is immediate, like the satisfaction you feel after checking something off your to-do list, and other times, it's long-term, like the health benefits of regular exercise. The reward gives your brain a reason to repeat the habit, strengthening the neural pathway associated with it. The stronger the reward, the more likely the habit will stick.

Habits are powerful because, once established, they require very little conscious thought or effort to maintain. Think about how you learned to drive a car. At first, every step—pressing the gas pedal, using the turn signal, checking the mirrors—required concentration. But over time, these actions became second nature. This is the brain's way of conserving energy. Once it recognizes a pattern, it automates the process, freeing up mental space for other tasks. This is both a blessing and a curse: it's great when the habit is positive, but it can work against you when the habit is negative.

The science behind habits also explains why they can be so difficult to change. Once a habit is formed, the neural pathways in the brain make it easier to repeat the behavior, even when you consciously want to stop. That's why bad habits, like mindlessly scrolling through social media or smoking, can feel so hard to break. But the good news is, understanding this cycle gives you the tools to rewire your brain. By identifying the cues and rewards that drive your habits, you can start to intentionally design new routines that support your goals.

One concept that's particularly useful when creating positive habits is the idea of **keystone habits**. These are foundational habits that have a ripple effect, leading to improvements in other areas of your life. For example, regular exercise is often considered a keystone habit because it not only improves physical health but also boosts mood, increases productivity, and promotes better sleep. By focusing on keystone habits, you can create a domino effect of positive change, making it easier to build other healthy habits along the way.

When you're starting the process of building a new habit, it's important to **start small**. The brain is more likely to resist big, sudden changes, which is why grand resolutions often fail. Instead, begin with a small, manageable version of the habit you want to create. If you're trying to establish a habit of daily exercise, for example, start with just 5 minutes of movement each day. This small commitment reduces the resistance and helps you establish the routine. Once the habit is in place, you can gradually build on it, increasing the time and intensity.

Repetition is key to turning a behavior into a habit. Every time you repeat the action, the neural pathway associated with that habit gets stronger, making the behavior more automatic. Research shows that it takes an average of 66 days to fully form a new habit, though this varies depending on the complexity of the habit and the individual. The key is to be patient and consistent, knowing that with each repetition, you're moving closer to making the habit a permanent part of your life.

In summary, understanding the science of habit formation is crucial for creating lasting positive habits. The habit loop—cue, routine, reward—explains why habits are formed and how they become automatic over time. By starting small, focusing on keystone habits, and repeating the behavior consistently, you can harness the power of your brain's natural tendencies to build habits that support your personal and professional growth. Once you understand how habits work, you hold the key to transforming your life, one small change at a time.

Identifying the Right Habits for Your Life

Creating positive habits is essential for personal growth, but it's even more important to ensure that the habits you build are aligned with your unique goals and values. Identifying the right habits for your life requires self-awareness and a deep understanding of what you want to achieve. Without this clarity, it's easy to get caught up in habits that don't truly serve your purpose or contribute to your overall well-being.

The first step in identifying the right habits is to start by assessing your **current habits**. Take a close look at your daily routines and behaviors. Which habits are helping you grow and move toward your goals? Which ones are holding you back? This process of reflection can reveal patterns that you may not have noticed before. For example, you might realize that your habit of checking your phone first thing in the morning sets a negative tone for the day, or that your evening walks help you clear your mind and reduce stress.

Once you've evaluated your current habits, it's time to think about the habits you need to **support your future growth**. This requires you to have a clear vision of where you want to go in life. What are your personal and professional goals? What kind of person do you want to become? These questions will guide you in determining which habits will bring you closer to that vision. For example, if your goal is to improve your health, habits like exercising regularly, eating nutritious meals, and getting enough sleep should become priorities. If your goal is to advance in your career, habits like learning new skills, networking, and staying organized might be key.

One effective way to approach this is to use the concept of **habit stacking**, where you build new habits on top of existing ones. This technique helps you integrate new behaviors into your life more seamlessly. For example, if you already have a habit of drinking coffee every morning, you could stack a new habit of journaling or reading a chapter of a self-development book during that time. By linking new habits to existing ones, you make it easier to remember and execute them consistently.

To identify the right habits, it's also important to think about the **areas of your life that need the most improvement**. Ask yourself: Where am I struggling? Where do I feel dissatisfied? This could be in your health, finances, relationships, or personal fulfillment. Often, these areas of dissatisfaction point to gaps in your habits. For instance, if you're constantly stressed and overwhelmed, you might need to develop habits that promote relaxation, such as meditation or scheduling regular breaks throughout your day.

Another key to identifying the right habits is to focus on the habits that align with your **core values**. Your values are the guiding principles that define what matters most to you. When your habits align with your values, they become more meaningful and easier to maintain. For example, if you value personal growth, habits like reading, reflecting, and setting goals will naturally fit into your life. If you value family, habits like spending quality time with loved ones or prioritizing family activities will feel more rewarding.

It's also essential to be **realistic** about the habits you choose to develop. Sometimes, we set ourselves up for failure by trying to adopt habits that are too ambitious or unsustainable. While it's great to aim high, it's equally important to be honest with yourself about what's feasible in your current lifestyle. Instead of aiming to run 10 miles every day if you're new to fitness, start with something manageable like a 15-minute walk. The goal is to create habits that you can stick with over the long term, not ones that lead to burnout or frustration.

Finally, consider the **long-term impact** of the habits you want to build. Ask yourself: How will this habit affect my life in a year? In five years? Positive habits compound over time, leading to significant growth and transformation, while negative habits can have the opposite effect. By keeping the long-term benefits in mind, you'll be more motivated to stay committed to the habits that truly matter.

In summary, identifying the right habits for your life starts with a clear understanding of your goals, values, and areas for improvement. By evaluating your current habits, aligning new habits with your vision for the future, and being realistic about what you can maintain, you can create a solid foundation for growth. Habits that are meaningful, sustainable, and aligned with your values will not only help you achieve your goals but also lead to a more fulfilling and balanced life.

Breaking Bad Habits

While building positive habits is essential for personal growth, breaking bad habits is just as important. Bad habits, whether they're minor distractions or deeply ingrained behaviors, can sabotage your progress and keep you from reaching your full potential. The key to breaking these habits is to understand why they exist and how to disrupt the cycle that keeps them alive.

Bad habits don't form out of nowhere—they are often the result of an automatic response to certain cues in your environment. Just like positive habits, bad habits follow the same cycle of **cue,**

routine, and reward. For example, if you're in the habit of snacking mindlessly while watching TV, the cue might be sitting down on the couch, the routine is reaching for a bag of chips, and the reward is the temporary satisfaction you get from eating. Over time, this behavior becomes automatic, and breaking it requires disrupting this cycle.

The first step in breaking a bad habit is to **identify the cue** that triggers it. Pay close attention to the situations, emotions, or environments that lead to the unwanted behavior. Are you stressed when you bite your nails? Bored when you scroll through social media for hours? By pinpointing the specific cues, you gain clarity on what sets the habit in motion. Once you've identified the cue, you can begin to consciously avoid or modify it. For instance, if stress is your cue for overeating, you can find alternative ways to manage stress, such as practicing deep breathing or going for a walk.

Next, it's crucial to **replace the routine**. Simply trying to eliminate a bad habit without replacing it with a healthier behavior rarely works because the brain still craves the reward associated with the habit. Instead of focusing solely on stopping the behavior, think about what you can do instead. For example, if you want to break the habit of checking your phone first thing in the morning, you might replace that routine with a more positive one, like journaling or stretching. This way, you're still addressing the underlying need for a morning routine, but in a way that supports your goals rather than detracts from them.

One powerful tool for breaking bad habits is to **change your environment**. The spaces we occupy have a profound influence on our behavior, and often, simply altering our surroundings can make it easier to break unwanted habits. If your bad habit is eating junk food late at night, for instance, keeping unhealthy snacks out of your home removes the temptation and makes it harder to engage in the behavior. Similarly, if your habit is procrastination, creating a workspace that is free of distractions, like social media or clutter, can help you stay focused.

Another critical aspect of breaking bad habits is understanding the **psychological rewards** they provide. Every bad habit serves a purpose, even if it's temporary relief from stress, boredom, or anxiety. To successfully break a habit, it's important to find a new, healthier reward that can satisfy the same need. For example, if you smoke cigarettes to relieve stress, you might replace that habit with deep breathing exercises or meditation, both of which can provide relaxation without the harmful effects of smoking.

It's also important to recognize that **willpower alone is often not enough** to break a bad habit. While it's tempting to rely on sheer determination, habits are deeply ingrained in the brain, and relying solely on willpower can lead to frustration and failure, especially in stressful or challenging moments. Instead, focus on creating systems and environments that make it easier to succeed. This might involve setting up routines that support your goal, such as preparing healthy meals in advance to avoid unhealthy snacking or scheduling time in your day for activities that help you de-stress.

Accountability is another powerful tool in breaking bad habits. Sharing your goal with someone else—whether it's a friend, family member, or coach—creates an added layer of responsibility. Knowing that someone else is aware of your efforts can increase your motivation to stay on track. Additionally, having someone who checks in on your progress can help you navigate challenges and celebrate small victories along the way.

Finally, it's important to **practice self-compassion** throughout the process. Breaking a bad habit doesn't happen overnight, and setbacks are a normal part of the journey. Instead of beating yourself up when you slip, acknowledge the mistake, learn from it, and refocus on your goal. Recognize that change takes time, and every small step forward is progress. By being kind to yourself and staying committed, you can make lasting changes without the burden of guilt or frustration.

In summary, breaking bad habits requires understanding the cues and rewards that drive them, and consciously replacing the routine with a healthier alternative. Changing your environment, seeking accountability, and practicing self-compassion can all help you stay on track. By approaching the process with patience and persistence, you can free yourself from habits that hold you back and create space for positive growth in your life.

Building Momentum with Small Wins

One of the most powerful ways to create lasting change and break free from bad habits is by focusing on small, manageable victories. These "small wins" help build momentum, encouraging you to keep pushing forward. Often, when we try to change a behavior, we aim for major transformations right away, setting ourselves up for frustration when progress feels slow or unattainable. But when you focus on small, achievable goals, each success adds to your confidence and resilience, making it easier to sustain long-term change.

Think of small wins as the building blocks of larger success. They may seem insignificant at first, but over time, they compound, creating a snowball effect that leads to major transformations. For instance, if your goal is to stop procrastinating, a small win could be dedicating just five minutes a day to a task you've been putting off. It might not seem like much, but those five minutes will add up, and soon, you'll find that you're building the habit of tackling tasks without delay.

The power of small wins lies in their ability to create **positive feedback loops**. Each time you achieve a small goal, you get a sense of accomplishment that boosts your motivation to keep going. This sense of progress is essential for maintaining focus and avoiding the discouragement that often comes when goals feel too big or distant. For example, if you're trying to improve your physical fitness, committing to a short daily workout, even just 10 minutes, can give you a sense of achievement that motivates you to gradually increase the intensity or duration of your exercises.

By setting yourself up for small, attainable victories, you also avoid the **perfectionist trap**—the idea that you need to achieve massive success right away or that any slip-up means total failure. When you embrace small wins, you allow yourself to celebrate progress instead of waiting for some far-off milestone. This approach fosters a growth mindset, where you recognize that each step, no matter how small, is part of a larger journey toward your goals.

One of the key benefits of small wins is that they help you build **consistency**. Consistency is the backbone of any habit change. Even if your efforts seem minimal at first, what matters most is that you're taking action regularly. Consistency helps rewire your brain and reinforce the new habits you're working to create. For example, if you want to break the habit of negative thinking, practicing small shifts in perspective—like replacing one negative thought a day with a positive one—can gradually lead to a more optimistic outlook over time. The small, consistent action becomes the foundation for a larger mental transformation.

Another reason small wins are effective is because they help you manage **willpower**. Willpower is a finite resource, and trying to force massive changes all at once can quickly deplete it. By focusing on small, manageable actions, you preserve your willpower, making it easier to stay committed over the long term. Small wins require less effort but still move you toward your desired outcome, allowing you to maintain momentum without feeling overwhelmed or drained. For instance, if you're trying to stop a habit like overeating, starting with smaller portions at one meal a day can help you gradually adjust your appetite and eating patterns, without the pressure of making an all-or-nothing change right away.

The beauty of small wins is that they are highly **customizable**. What constitutes a small win will differ for everyone, depending on your starting point and your goals. The key is to identify small steps that are meaningful to you. If you're struggling to save money, a small win might be skipping your daily coffee purchase once a week and putting that money into savings instead. If you're trying to reduce screen time, a small win could be setting a timer to limit social media use for 10 minutes less each day. The more tailored your small wins are to your personal habits and challenges, the more effective they'll be in helping you build momentum.

To ensure the effectiveness of small wins, it's helpful to **track your progress**. Keeping a simple record of your daily victories can provide a visual reminder of how far you've come, even when the changes feel gradual. Whether it's checking off a daily habit in a planner or using an app to track your goals, seeing tangible evidence of your progress can give you the extra motivation to keep going. Tracking also helps you stay accountable, reminding you to prioritize the small actions that will eventually lead to big results.

In summary, small wins are a powerful tool for breaking bad habits and building positive ones. They allow you to make consistent progress, preserve willpower, and stay motivated by celebrating each step forward. By focusing on manageable, achievable goals, you can create a strong foundation for long-term change, and over time, these small victories will compound into significant growth.

Turning Setbacks into Stepping Stones

No journey of personal growth is without setbacks. When trying to break bad habits or build positive ones, you'll inevitably face challenges. What separates those who succeed from those who give up is how they respond to these setbacks. Instead of viewing mistakes as failures, successful people see them as valuable learning experiences. The key to long-term change isn't avoiding setbacks altogether—it's knowing how to turn them into stepping stones for future success.

When you encounter a setback, the first step is to **reframe your perspective**. It's easy to fall into the trap of negative thinking when things don't go as planned. You might feel frustrated, disappointed, or even guilty. However, these emotions, while natural, can hold you back if you let them take control. Instead of focusing on the setback as a failure, ask yourself, "What can I learn from this?" Shifting your mindset from failure to growth helps you see the setback as a temporary detour rather than a dead end.

For example, let's say you're working on breaking the habit of procrastination, and one day you fall back into old patterns, spending hours avoiding an important task. Instead of beating yourself up for not being perfect, take a step back and analyze what led to the setback. Did you feel overwhelmed by the task?

Were there distractions you didn't account for? By identifying the factors that contributed to the slip-up, you can take steps to address them in the future, turning the setback into a learning opportunity.

Another essential part of overcoming setbacks is to **practice self-compassion**. Many people are harder on themselves than they would ever be on someone else. When you make a mistake, it's common to spiral into self-criticism, telling yourself things like "I'll never change" or "I'm not strong enough to break this habit." But self-compassion is crucial for bouncing back from setbacks. Instead of criticizing yourself, treat yourself with the same kindness you would offer a friend. Acknowledge that change is hard and that everyone faces obstacles along the way.

By treating yourself with compassion, you create the emotional space to try again without the weight of guilt or shame. This doesn't mean excusing your behavior, but rather recognizing that setbacks are a normal part of the process. Remember, the goal isn't perfection—it's progress. Each time you stumble, you have an opportunity to get back up and keep moving forward.

Next, it's important to **develop resilience** by building strategies to prevent future setbacks. Once you've analyzed the reasons for a setback, you can make adjustments to your plan. This might involve tweaking your environment, modifying your goals, or finding new ways to stay accountable. If you're trying to break the habit of staying up too late, for instance, and you find yourself slipping back into that pattern, you might start setting an earlier alarm or establishing a more structured bedtime routine. By proactively addressing the triggers that lead to setbacks, you reduce the likelihood of repeating the same mistakes.

Setbacks also offer the chance to **reevaluate your goals**. Sometimes, setbacks occur because the goal you've set is too ambitious or unrealistic. If you find yourself consistently struggling, it may be time to adjust your expectations. For example, if you're trying to establish a daily exercise routine but keep missing your target, it might be more realistic to start with three days a week and gradually increase. Adjusting your goals doesn't mean you're lowering your standards—it means you're being smart about creating a plan that's sustainable in the long run.

Another helpful strategy is to **seek support** when you face setbacks. Sharing your challenges with someone else—a friend, mentor, or coach—can provide valuable insights and encouragement. Other people can offer a fresh perspective, help you see the progress you've made, and remind you of your overall goal when you feel discouraged. Sometimes, just talking through the setback can help you gain clarity and find solutions you hadn't considered on your own. Support from others can also hold you accountable and keep you motivated to keep trying, even after a setback.

Finally, it's essential to **celebrate your resilience** when you overcome a setback. Every time you pick yourself back up and continue working toward your goal, you build strength and resilience. Recognize the effort you're putting into your personal growth and give yourself credit for not giving up. It's easy to focus on what went wrong, but it's equally important to acknowledge the courage it takes to keep moving forward despite obstacles.

In the grand scheme of personal development, setbacks are not failures—they are stepping stones that help you grow stronger, wiser, and more resilient. Each time you face a challenge, you have the opportunity to learn something new about yourself and refine your approach. The road to lasting change is rarely a straight line, but every twist and turn brings you closer to your goal. By embracing setbacks as part of the journey, practicing self-compassion, and staying committed to your progress, you can transform temporary obstacles into powerful stepping stones toward a better, more fulfilling life.

{ 5 }

Chapter 5: Managing Time Effectively

Identifying Priorities Through Reflection
Managing time effectively starts with a clear understanding of what truly matters in your life. Before diving into time management techniques, it's essential to pause and reflect on your core values, long-term goals, and the activities that align with those priorities. Time is a finite resource, and if we're not intentional about how we use it, we can easily get caught up in tasks that don't contribute to our overall well-being or success. This reflection process is the foundation upon which effective time management is built.

To begin, ask yourself: What are my core values? These are the principles and beliefs that guide your actions and decisions. They could include things like family, health, career success, personal growth, or giving back to your community. Identifying your values helps you prioritize tasks that align with them, ensuring that your time is spent on what truly matters.

For example, if family is one of your core values, but you find yourself consistently working late and missing important family events, there's a disconnect between how you're spending your time and what's important to you. Reflecting on this can prompt you to adjust your schedule, set boundaries at work, or make other changes to bring your time usage in line with your values.

Once you've identified your values, it's time to think about your **long-term goals**. What do you want to achieve in the next year, five years, or even ten years? Your goals might include things like advancing in your career, starting a business, getting in shape, writing a book, or traveling the world. Whatever they are, they should be clear, specific, and aligned with your values. If your goals are vague or undefined, it's easy to get lost in the day-to-day grind without making meaningful progress.

A helpful exercise is to write down your top five goals and then rank them in order of importance. This process forces you to confront what's most significant to you and helps you see where your time should be focused. For instance, if your top goal is to start your own business, but you're spending most of your free time on activities unrelated to that goal, it's time to rethink how you're allocating your time. By regularly reflecting on your goals and their importance, you'll be better equipped to make decisions that move you closer to achieving them.

Another crucial aspect of reflection is evaluating your **current time use**. It's one thing to set goals and identify values, but how you spend your time on a day-to-day basis may not reflect those priorities. A practical exercise is to track your activities for a week. Write down everything you do, from the moment you wake up to the time you go to bed. This might sound tedious, but it can be incredibly eye-opening. At the end of the week, review your time log and ask yourself some important questions: How much time did I spend on activities that align with my values and goals? How much time was spent on distractions or low-value tasks? Where are the gaps between what I say is important and how I actually spend my time?

For example, if one of your goals is to improve your health, but your time log shows that you barely exercised and spent hours each day on social media, you have clear evidence that your time is not being used effectively. Reflection is about facing these truths head-on, without judgment, and using them to make intentional changes moving forward.

Finally, reflection also helps you identify and eliminate **distractions** that steal your time. Distractions can come in many forms—social media, email, TV, or even well-meaning friends and family who unknowingly pull you away from your priorities. When you reflect on your time use, it becomes easier to spot these distractions and make a conscious effort to reduce or eliminate them. For example, if you find that you're spending hours a day scrolling through social media with little benefit, you might decide to limit your social media use to specific times of the day or set a timer to remind yourself when it's time to get back to work.

In conclusion, identifying your priorities through reflection is the first and most critical step in managing your time effectively. By aligning your daily activities with your core values and long-term goals, and by becoming aware of how you're currently using your time, you set yourself up for success. Time management isn't just about being more productive—it's about ensuring that the time you do spend is meaningful and moves you toward the life you truly want to live.

The Power of Time Blocking and Scheduling

Once you've identified your priorities and reflected on how your current time use aligns with them, the next step is to implement a system that helps you manage your time effectively. One of the most powerful tools for this is **time blocking**—a simple yet highly effective method of organizing your day by allocating specific blocks of time to different tasks. Time blocking allows you to focus on one activity at a time, reduces distractions, and ensures that you're dedicating enough time to your top priorities.

Time blocking works because it creates a structured plan for your day, allowing you to take control of your time instead of reacting to whatever comes your way. Rather than letting your day be dictated by random tasks, interruptions, or distractions, you set aside dedicated blocks of time for the things that matter most. It's like creating a daily blueprint that ensures your goals and priorities are given the time and attention they deserve.

To start, think about your daily tasks and responsibilities—both personal and professional. Make a list of the things you need to get done regularly, such as work projects, exercise, family time, or even self-care activities like reading or meditation. Then, use a planner or digital calendar to assign specific blocks of time to each task. For example, you might dedicate 9:00 AM to 11:00 AM for focused work on a big project, 12:00 PM to 1:00 PM for lunch and a walk, and 2:00 PM to 3:00 PM for meetings or answering emails.

The beauty of time blocking is that it brings **intentionality** to your schedule. By planning your day in advance, you're less likely to waste time or get sidetracked by unimportant tasks. It also helps you set clear boundaries for when you'll focus on different areas of your life. For instance, if you've blocked off 6:00 PM to 7:00 PM for family time, you know that's a sacred hour where work emails and other distractions take a back seat.

One of the biggest benefits of time blocking is that it helps you avoid **multitasking**, which is often a major time-waster. Many people believe they're being more efficient when they juggle multiple tasks at once, but research shows the opposite is true. Multitasking divides your attention, reduces productivity, and increases the likelihood of mistakes. With time blocking, you're focused on one task at a time, giving it your full attention. This allows you to complete tasks more quickly and efficiently while producing higher-quality work.

For example, instead of answering emails sporadically throughout the day, you might block off a specific time in the morning and afternoon to handle all of your emails in one go. This way, you're not constantly interrupting your flow to check your inbox, and you can dedicate uninterrupted time to more important tasks, like working on a big project or brainstorming new ideas.

Another key advantage of time blocking is that it helps you build **consistency** in your routine. When you set aside the same block of time each day or week for important tasks, those activities become habits. For example, if you block off 7:00 AM to 8:00 AM every morning for exercise, it becomes a non-negotiable part of your routine. Over time, this consistency leads to greater discipline and ensures that your most important activities don't get pushed aside by less critical tasks.

While time blocking is highly effective, it's important to remember that life is unpredictable, and things don't always go according to plan. That's why your schedule should have some **flexibility** built in. If something urgent comes up and you need to rearrange your time blocks, that's okay. The goal isn't to stick rigidly to your schedule at all costs, but rather to have a structure in place that guides your day. If a meeting runs late or an unexpected issue arises, simply adjust your time blocks as needed and return to your plan once things settle down.

Another helpful tip when time blocking is to include **breaks** in your schedule. Working nonstop can lead to burnout and decreased productivity. By blocking off time for short breaks throughout the day, you give your brain a chance to recharge, allowing you to return to your tasks with more focus and energy. For instance, after two hours of deep work, you might schedule a 15-minute break to stretch, grab a snack, or take a walk. These small breaks not only improve your productivity but also contribute to your overall well-being.

In addition to daily time blocks, consider creating a **weekly schedule** that includes time for both work and personal activities. For example, you might dedicate Monday mornings to big-picture planning, Tuesday afternoons to team meetings, and Fridays to wrapping up loose ends. On a personal level, you might block off Saturday afternoons for family outings or Sunday evenings for self-reflection and goal-setting for the week ahead. A weekly schedule helps you maintain a balanced approach to time management, ensuring that you're making time for both professional and personal growth.

In conclusion, time blocking and scheduling are essential tools for managing your time effectively. By planning your day and week in advance, focusing on one task at a time, and creating a consistent routine, you'll maximize your productivity and ensure that your most important goals are getting the attention they deserve. Time blocking empowers you to take control of your schedule, reduce distractions, and create a more fulfilling, balanced life.

Overcoming Procrastination and Time-Wasters

No matter how organized your schedule is, procrastination can easily undermine even the best-laid plans. It's one of the most common barriers to effective time management, and overcoming it requires a conscious effort. Procrastination isn't simply about laziness or lack of discipline—often, it's rooted in deeper psychological factors like fear of failure, perfectionism, or feeling overwhelmed. Understanding why you procrastinate is the first step toward overcoming it, and there are practical strategies to help you break free from its grip.

Let's begin by addressing the **underlying reasons for procrastination**. At its core, procrastination often stems from a discomfort with the task at hand. You might avoid starting a project because it feels too big or complex, or you may worry that you won't do it perfectly. These feelings create anxiety, which leads to avoidance. Instead of tackling the task, you might distract yourself with something easier—scrolling through social media, organizing your desk, or even working on a different, less important task.

Recognizing this avoidance pattern is key to breaking free. Start by acknowledging the emotions that cause you to procrastinate. Are you avoiding the task because it feels overwhelming? Are you afraid of not meeting your own expectations or those of others? Once you've identified the root cause, you can begin to address it directly. For example, if a project feels too large, break it down into smaller, more manageable steps. By tackling just one small part at a time, you'll reduce the anxiety associated with the task and make it easier to start.

One effective strategy for overcoming procrastination is the "two-minute rule." This simple technique involves starting any task that can be done in two minutes or less, right away. The idea is that once you begin something, you're more likely to keep going. If the task is more complex, the two-minute rule can still help by encouraging you to take the first small step. For instance, if you need to write a report but are procrastinating, commit to spending just two minutes outlining the introduction. Often, once you get started, you'll find it easier to continue, and the momentum will carry you forward.

Another powerful tool to combat procrastination is the **Pomodoro Technique**. This time management method encourages you to work in short, focused bursts with regular breaks. Set a timer for 25 minutes (a "Pomodoro") and focus entirely on one task for that time. Once the timer goes off, take a five-minute break before starting another Pomodoro. After four Pomodoros, take a longer break of 15-30 minutes. This technique works because it makes large tasks feel less daunting and encourages deep focus for short periods, which helps you build momentum. It also offers regular breaks, which prevent burnout and keep your mind fresh.

Procrastination often leads to **time-wasting behaviors**, such as getting lost in social media, browsing the internet aimlessly, or multitasking. These activities might feel productive in the moment, but they steal valuable time and reduce overall efficiency. One of the first steps to reducing time-wasting is to **track how you currently spend your time**. Use a time-tracking app or simply jot down what you're doing throughout the day. This will give you a clear picture of where your time is going and help you identify patterns of procrastination and distraction.

Once you're aware of your time-wasters, take steps to minimize them. For instance, if social media is a major distraction, consider setting time limits on your apps or scheduling specific times in the day for social media use. You could also use website blockers that prevent access to distracting sites during work hours. If email or messaging apps are pulling you away from important tasks, designate certain times of the day to check and respond to messages, rather than allowing them to interrupt your flow continuously.

Another common source of lost time is **multitasking**. While it may seem efficient to juggle multiple tasks at once, research shows that multitasking actually reduces productivity and increases the likelihood of errors. When you switch between tasks, your brain needs time to adjust, which creates mental "lag" and diminishes focus. Instead of multitasking, practice **single-tasking**—dedicating your full attention to one task at a time. You'll find that you complete tasks more quickly and with better quality when you're fully focused.

An often-overlooked aspect of procrastination is the pressure to be **perfect**. Many people delay starting a task because they want to ensure it's done flawlessly. However, perfectionism can be paralyzing. It creates unrealistic standards that make the task seem impossible to complete, leading to avoidance. To overcome perfectionism, remind yourself that done is better than perfect. Focus on progress, not perfection. Allow yourself to make mistakes, knowing that you can always go back and improve your work later. This shift in mindset can dramatically reduce procrastination and help you move forward.

In addition to these strategies, it's important to **create a supportive environment** that minimizes distractions. Designate a quiet, organized workspace where you can focus without interruptions. Turn off notifications on your phone and computer during work periods, and let others know when you're unavailable to ensure uninterrupted focus. By setting up an environment that supports your goals, you'll be less likely to procrastinate and waste time.

In conclusion, procrastination and time-wasters can sabotage even the best time management efforts, but with the right strategies, you can overcome them. By understanding the root causes of procrastination, using techniques like the two-minute rule and the Pomodoro Technique, and eliminating distractions and multitasking, you can reclaim your time and focus on what truly matters. Breaking free from procrastination is not about working harder; it's about working smarter and developing habits that allow you to make consistent progress toward your goals.

Prioritizing Tasks with the Eisenhower Matrix

Effectively managing your time requires more than just identifying how you spend it—you also need to determine which tasks truly deserve your attention. One of the best tools for doing this is the **Eisenhower Matrix**, a decision-making framework that helps you prioritize tasks based on their urgency and importance. Named after former U.S. President Dwight D. Eisenhower, this simple yet powerful matrix encourages you to categorize tasks into four distinct quadrants, allowing you to focus on what matters most and avoid wasting time on less meaningful activities.

The Eisenhower Matrix divides tasks into four quadrants:

1. **Urgent and Important**: Tasks in this quadrant require immediate attention. These are the tasks that must be done right away because they have clear deadlines or significant consequences if delayed. For example, a pressing work project due by the end of the day or an unexpected family emergency would fall into this category. These tasks often represent crises or problems that need to be solved as soon as possible.

2. **Not Urgent but Important**: Tasks in this quadrant are crucial for long-term success, but they don't have immediate deadlines. This includes activities like planning, goal setting, personal development, and relationship-building. These tasks are often neglected in favor of more urgent matters, but they are the key to sustainable growth and progress. For example, spending time learning a new skill,

exercising, or creating a strategic plan for your business are all important but not urgent.

3. **Urgent but Not Important**: These tasks demand your immediate attention, but they don't contribute much to your long-term goals or success. They are often interruptions or activities that are urgent for others but not necessarily for you. For instance, answering non-critical emails, attending meetings that don't align with your priorities, or dealing with minor issues that could be delegated. It's easy to get trapped in this quadrant, as these tasks feel pressing, but they often prevent you from focusing on more important work.

4. **Not Urgent and Not Important**: This final quadrant contains tasks that are neither time-sensitive nor valuable. These activities often represent distractions or time-wasters, such as excessive social media use, watching TV, or engaging in unproductive habits. While it's fine to engage in some of these activities for relaxation, spending too much time in this quadrant can detract from your productivity and personal growth.

To effectively use the Eisenhower Matrix, start by **listing all your current tasks**. Then, categorize each task into one of the four quadrants. This process forces you to evaluate what truly matters and what's simply consuming your time without adding value. Once you've organized your tasks, you'll have a clear picture of where to focus your energy and where to cut back.

Let's break down how to tackle each quadrant:

For tasks that are **urgent and important**, these should be your top priority. These are the things you need to focus on immediately. However, living in this quadrant for too long can lead to stress and burnout, as you're constantly putting out fires. To avoid this, try to minimize the number of tasks that end up in this quadrant by planning ahead and addressing important tasks before they become urgent.

Tasks that are **important but not urgent** are where you should spend the majority of your time. These activities are essential for long-term success, and the more time you devote to them, the fewer crises you'll face in the future. Unfortunately, these tasks often get pushed aside in favor of urgent matters. To prevent this, schedule time in your day or week specifically for these activities. For example, set aside time each morning for personal development, exercise, or strategic planning. Treat this time as non-negotiable to ensure these important tasks don't get crowded out by urgent but less important ones.

For tasks that are **urgent but not important**, your goal should be to **delegate or eliminate** them whenever possible. If someone else can handle the task, delegate it. If the task doesn't need to be done at all, eliminate it from your schedule. It's important to recognize that just because a task is urgent doesn't mean you're the one who has to handle it. By learning to delegate effectively, you free up time for more meaningful work.

Finally, tasks that are **neither urgent nor important** should be minimized or avoided altogether. These are the time-wasters that often sneak into our day and steal valuable time without contributing to our goals. If you find yourself spending too much time in this quadrant, consider setting limits. For example, you might limit social media use to 30 minutes a day or allocate specific times for leisure activities. Being aware of how much time you spend on non-essential activities can help you reclaim those hours for more productive pursuits.

One of the biggest benefits of using the Eisenhower Matrix is that it helps you move from a **reactive** approach to a **proactive** approach to time management. Instead of constantly responding to urgent tasks and feeling overwhelmed by deadlines, you can plan your day with intention. By focusing on what's truly important, you'll make steady progress toward your long-term goals, while also reducing the stress that comes from last-minute rushes and avoidable crises.

Incorporating the Eisenhower Matrix into your daily routine will help you make better decisions about how to use your time. It enables you to prioritize effectively, delegate when necessary, and eliminate distractions that don't serve your goals. Over time, you'll find that you're able to focus more on what matters most and less on what simply feels urgent in the moment. This shift in mindset can dramatically improve your productivity and lead to greater satisfaction in both your personal and professional life.

In conclusion, the Eisenhower Matrix is a valuable tool for identifying and prioritizing tasks based on their urgency and importance. By categorizing your tasks and taking deliberate action to focus on the important ones, delegate the less critical, and minimize distractions, you'll develop a clearer, more purposeful approach to managing your time. This process helps you align your daily actions with your long-term goals, ensuring that you're making meaningful progress without getting lost in the chaos of day-to-day demands.

The Power of Time Blocking for Focus and Efficiency

In today's fast-paced world, distractions are everywhere, making it difficult to stay focused and productive. Whether it's constant emails, social media notifications, or the temptation to multitask, our attention is pulled in multiple directions, often leading to wasted time and reduced efficiency. One of the most effective ways to combat these distractions and take control of your day is through **time blocking**. Time blocking is a productivity technique that involves scheduling specific blocks of time for focused work on a single task or group of related tasks. By allocating dedicated time for each task, you can significantly enhance your focus, reduce distractions, and make better use of your time.

At its core, time blocking is about **being intentional with your schedule**. Instead of letting your day unfold haphazardly or reacting to the demands of others, you take control of your time by planning it in advance. Each block of time is reserved for a specific activity, whether it's working on a project, attending a meeting, exercising, or even taking a break. The key is to stick to the schedule as much as possible, focusing only on the task at hand during each block and avoiding interruptions.

One of the biggest advantages of time blocking is that it helps to **eliminate multitasking**, which is one of the main culprits of reduced productivity. While many people believe that multitasking allows them to get more done, research shows that it actually decreases efficiency and increases the likelihood of mistakes. The human brain isn't designed to focus on multiple tasks simultaneously; instead, it quickly switches back and forth between tasks, which leads to mental fatigue and reduced performance. By dedicating specific time blocks to single tasks, you allow your brain to fully concentrate on one thing at a time, leading to deeper focus and higher quality work.

To get started with time blocking, begin by **assessing your priorities and tasks**. Look at your to-do list and determine which tasks are most important or require the most focus. These tasks should be given priority in your time blocks. For example, if you have a major project due at the end of the week, block out time each day to work on it in focused intervals. Tasks that are less critical or require less concentration can be scheduled during times when you typically have lower energy or focus.

Next, **create a daily schedule** that includes time blocks for all your key activities. This doesn't mean every minute of your day needs to be rigidly structured—there's flexibility within the framework. For instance, you might block out 90 minutes in the morning for deep work on a creative project, followed by a 30-minute break, and then an hour for meetings or responding to emails. In the afternoon, you could block out time for exercise, administrative tasks, or catching up on reading. The goal is to ensure that your most important tasks have dedicated time in your day, and that you're not constantly switching between activities.

It's also important to **schedule breaks within your time blocks**. The brain can only focus deeply for a limited period before it starts to fatigue, so incorporating regular breaks is essential for maintaining productivity throughout the day. Techniques like the **Pomodoro Technique** (working for 25 minutes followed by a 5-minute break) or simply scheduling longer breaks after periods of deep work can help you stay fresh and avoid burnout. During these breaks, step away from your desk, stretch, or engage in an activity that relaxes your mind—this will help you recharge for the next time block.

Another critical aspect of time blocking is **protecting your time** from distractions and interruptions. This means being proactive about minimizing external interruptions during your time blocks. For instance, you can set your phone to "Do Not Disturb" mode, close unnecessary tabs on your computer, or let colleagues know you're unavailable during certain hours. Setting these boundaries ensures that you can fully immerse yourself in the task at hand without being derailed by distractions. You might also consider using tools like time-tracking apps to help you stay accountable and measure how effectively you're sticking to your time blocks.

As you implement time blocking into your routine, be prepared for some **trial and error**. It may take time to find the right balance between structured time and flexibility. You might discover that certain tasks take longer than expected or that unexpected events disrupt your schedule. That's okay. The beauty of time blocking is that it's adaptable. You can adjust your blocks as needed and experiment with different time intervals until you find a rhythm that works for you. The key is to maintain consistency and not abandon the practice if your schedule doesn't always go perfectly as planned.

One of the most profound benefits of time blocking is that it helps you **build momentum** throughout the day. When you complete one task within a designated time block, you gain a sense of accomplishment, which motivates you to tackle the next task. This momentum is crucial for maintaining productivity and staying on track with your goals. Additionally, because time blocking forces you to focus on one task at a time, you'll often find that you finish tasks more quickly and with higher quality than when you try to juggle multiple things at once.

Over time, time blocking can help you develop a **sense of control and mastery** over your schedule. Instead of feeling overwhelmed by an endless list of tasks, you'll have a clear plan for how to tackle them. You'll be able to allocate your time more efficiently, ensuring that important tasks are completed on time and without unnecessary stress. This sense of control can also lead to greater work-life balance, as you'll have dedicated time for both professional tasks and personal activities, making it easier to switch off at the end of the day.

In conclusion, time blocking is a powerful tool for managing your time more effectively. By scheduling dedicated blocks of time for focused work, eliminating distractions, and creating a structure that supports deep concentration, you can increase your productivity and achieve your goals more efficiently. The key is to be intentional with your time, protect it from interruptions, and continuously refine your schedule to suit your needs. With time blocking, you'll not only get more done, but you'll also experience a greater sense of control, focus, and satisfaction in both your personal and professional life.

Part 2: Elevating Your Professional Growth

Chapter 6: Defining Success in Your Career

Understanding What Success Means to You
Success in your career is a deeply personal concept. For some, it might mean climbing the corporate ladder and earning prestigious titles, while for others, it could mean achieving financial independence, work-life balance, or making a meaningful impact through their work. What's clear is that there is no one-size-fits-all definition of success, and trying to conform to society's standard view of it can often lead to dissatisfaction. The first step in defining career success is to take a step back and reflect on what it truly means to you, not just what you think it *should* mean.

Why Traditional Definitions May Not Fit Society tends to offer a narrow definition of professional success, usually revolving around wealth, status, or power. While these elements can be important to some, they don't necessarily guarantee fulfillment. Chasing someone else's idea of success can lead to frustration, burnout, or a sense of emptiness even after you've achieved what you thought you wanted.

For example, think about individuals who have worked hard to achieve high-ranking positions or amass large fortunes, only to feel unfulfilled once they arrive. What these stories often illustrate is that external markers of success—things like money, titles, or recognition—don't always align with internal satisfaction. The key is to stop and ask yourself, "What do I really want out of my career?" Defining your own version of success will help you set meaningful goals and make decisions that align with your values and desires.

Reflecting on Your Priorities Start by reflecting on your life and career up to this point. What moments have made you feel the most fulfilled? When have you felt truly proud of what you've achieved? These moments provide valuable clues about what really drives you and what you consider a meaningful accomplishment. Sometimes, the greatest feelings of success come from intangible experiences—like mentoring someone, solving a challenging problem, or achieving work-life harmony—rather than tangible rewards like promotions or bonuses.

A good way to begin is by asking yourself a few questions:

- What am I passionate about in my work?
- Which of my professional achievements have brought me the most joy?
- What does my ideal workday or work environment look like?
- What do I value most—freedom, creativity, stability, challenge, impact? These reflections will help you clarify what really matters to you, not just what you think is expected of you.

Recognizing External Influence It's easy to let outside forces influence your idea of success. Family expectations, societal pressures, and even social media can make you feel as if you're falling short unless you meet certain benchmarks. However, these external pressures often don't take into account your unique goals or aspirations. Recognizing this influence is crucial because it allows you to separate what others might expect from what you truly want.

For instance, if you find yourself striving for a job with a high salary simply because it's what others around you value, take a moment to ask yourself if financial gain is truly your driving force. Perhaps what you're really seeking is more freedom, creative expression, or the ability to make a positive impact in your community. The clearer you are about your motivations, the more you can focus on building a career that serves you—not the expectations of others.

Creating a Personalized Career Vision Once you've taken the time to reflect, it's time to start forming a **personalized career vision**. This is a broad outline of what success looks like for you in both the short term and the long term. It doesn't have to be rigid or set in stone—life circumstances change, and so will your goals—but it should be rooted in your passions, values, and priorities.

For some, this might mean pursuing leadership roles or entrepreneurship. For others, it could mean seeking balance between work and personal life, or working in a field that aligns with a cause they're passionate about. Whatever your path, the goal is to make sure that your career aligns with who you are and what you care about, rather than what others think you should care about.

Embracing Your Unique Path Finally, remember that your career is your own journey, and it's okay if it looks different from those around you. Success doesn't need to follow a linear or conventional path. You might take risks, make pivots, or pursue opportunities that others don't understand. That's perfectly fine, as long as you're building a career that brings you satisfaction and aligns with your definition of success.

In the end, **defining success in your career** is about deeply understanding what matters to you, embracing your individuality, and creating a vision that guides your decisions and actions. By doing this, you set yourself up for not just professional achievements, but genuine fulfillment in your work life.

Setting Specific, Measurable Career Goals

Once you have defined what success looks like for you, the next step is to turn that vision into actionable goals. Defining success is the foundation, but without clear goals, your career path can become unfocused. Setting specific, measurable goals provides you with a roadmap to guide your progress, helping you stay on course while ensuring that your efforts are aligned with your personal definition of success.

The Power of Setting Intentional Goals When you set career goals, you give yourself direction and purpose. Goals act like a compass—they help you navigate the complexities of your professional life by focusing your energy on what truly matters. The key is to ensure that these goals are not just broad desires, like "I want to be successful," but instead, clearly defined steps toward that success.

For example, rather than saying, "I want to grow in my career," a more actionable goal would be, "I want to gain the skills necessary to lead a team within the next two years." This is much more focused and gives you a concrete outcome to work toward. The more intentional your goals are, the easier it becomes to measure your progress and stay motivated.

The SMART Goals Framework One of the most effective ways to create clear career goals is by using the **SMART goals framework**. SMART stands for Specific, Measurable, Achievable, Relevant, and Time-bound. Let's break down how each of these elements works:

- **Specific:** Your goal should be clear and precise, leaving no room for ambiguity. Ask yourself, "What exactly do I want to accomplish?" A vague goal like "I want to do well in my career" should be refined into something more concrete, such as "I want to become a project manager in my company's marketing department."
- **Measurable:** You should be able to track your progress and know when you've reached your goal. For example, if your goal is to gain new skills, you could set measurable milestones, such as completing three online courses in your field or obtaining a specific certification.
- **Achievable:** While it's important to challenge yourself, your goals should still be realistic. Ask yourself if you have the resources, time, and ability to achieve your goal. Setting an overly ambitious goal can lead to frustration and burnout. Break larger goals into smaller, more manageable steps to ensure they are within reach.
- **Relevant:** Your goal should align with your broader career aspirations. If your long-term success is defined by leadership, focus on goals that enhance leadership skills, rather than unrelated objectives. Every goal should contribute to your overall vision of success.
- **Time-bound:** A goal needs a deadline or time frame. This helps create a sense of urgency and ensures that you stay accountable. For instance, instead of saying, "I want to improve my networking skills," you could set a time-bound goal like, "I will attend two professional networking events per month for the next six months."

Breaking Down Long-Term and Short-Term Goals Career goals can be divided into two main categories: **long-term goals** and **short-term goals**. Both are important and should complement each other.

- **Long-term goals** are the big-picture aspirations, the milestones you hope to achieve in several years. These could be things like becoming a department head, starting your own business, or transitioning into a new industry. Long-term goals require sustained effort and often involve multiple steps to reach.
- **Short-term goals**, on the other hand, are the smaller, more immediate steps you can take to move closer to your long-term goals. These might include learning a specific skill, gaining a certain amount of work experience, or expanding your professional network. Short-term goals serve as building blocks for achieving your broader aspirations.

For example, if your long-term goal is to move into a leadership position, your short-term goals could include taking on more responsibility in your current role, enrolling in leadership training, or seeking out a mentor. Each of these short-term steps brings you closer to your ultimate vision of success.

Tracking Progress and Staying Motivated Setting goals is only half the battle; the other half is staying committed to them. One of the best ways to maintain momentum is to **track your progress**. Regularly checking in on your goals allows you to see how far you've come and what adjustments, if any, need to be made.

To do this, consider setting up periodic reviews—monthly or quarterly—where you reflect on your achievements and reassess your next steps. If you're not where you want to be, don't get discouraged. Use setbacks as learning opportunities and refine your approach. This practice of continuous reflection and adjustment will help you stay focused on the bigger picture while adapting to changing circumstances.

Another important aspect of goal-setting is finding ways to stay motivated. Celebrate your achievements, no matter how small. When you reach a milestone or accomplish a goal, take a moment to acknowledge your hard work and reward yourself. This positive reinforcement will keep you energized and driven to continue working toward your larger goals.

Adjusting Your Goals as You Grow It's also important to remember that goals are not static. As you grow in your career and as your priorities evolve, your goals may need to change as well. What you once considered an important milestone might no longer align with your vision of success. Don't be afraid to adjust your goals to better fit your current situation and aspirations. Flexibility is key to long-term success, as it allows you to adapt to new opportunities and challenges.

By setting specific, measurable, and achievable goals, you can ensure that every step you take is purposeful and aligned with your career vision. Tracking progress, celebrating achievements, and remaining flexible are all essential to staying motivated on the journey toward professional success. Through intentional goal-setting, you can turn your vision of success into a reality.

Identifying and Leveraging Your Strengths

One of the most important steps in defining and achieving success in your career is to have a clear understanding of your strengths. These are the skills, talents, and qualities that set you apart and allow you to excel in your work. Identifying and leveraging your strengths not only enhances your performance but also brings a sense of satisfaction and fulfillment. When you focus on what you do best, you create a natural alignment between your abilities and your career goals, which makes the journey toward success smoother and more enjoyable.

Why Knowing Your Strengths Matters Understanding your strengths is key to setting yourself up for success. Imagine trying to build a career without being aware of what you naturally excel at—it's like trying to drive a car without knowing how to steer. You may make progress, but it will be a struggle. On the other hand, when you know your strengths, you can align your career choices with what you are naturally good at, which leads to greater productivity and higher satisfaction.

Moreover, recognizing your strengths helps you build confidence. When you are aware of what you do well, you're more likely to seek out opportunities that play to your abilities. This not only boosts your performance but also increases your sense of competence and self-assurance, which are crucial for career growth.

How to Identify Your Strengths If you're unsure about your strengths, there are several ways to discover them. The first step is self-reflection. Take some time to think about the tasks or projects that you've enjoyed the most in your career or personal life. When were you at your best? What kind of work felt effortless, even enjoyable? These moments of ease and enjoyment are often signals of your strengths.

In addition to self-reflection, consider seeking feedback from colleagues, supervisors, or mentors. Sometimes, others can see strengths in us that we may overlook. Ask those who know your work to share their thoughts on what they believe you excel at. You might be surprised by the insights you receive.

You can also use assessments like the StrengthsFinder test or the Myers-Briggs Type Indicator, which are designed to help individuals identify their natural talents and preferences. These tools can provide valuable insights into your strengths, helping you to better understand how you can use them to your advantage in your career.

Playing to Your Strengths in Your Career Once you've identified your strengths, the next step is to figure out how to leverage them effectively in your career. This means aligning your daily work, projects, and long-term goals with what you're naturally good at.

For example, if one of your strengths is communication, seek opportunities where you can use that skill, such as leading presentations, mentoring others, or handling client interactions. If you're strong in analytical thinking, look for roles that allow you to solve complex problems or create strategies. By focusing on work that plays to your strengths, you not only improve your performance but also find more enjoyment in what you do.

Additionally, recognizing your strengths can help you identify areas for growth. While it's important to leverage your existing skills, it's equally important to continue developing new ones that complement your strengths. For instance, if you're great at problem-solving but struggle with time management, working on your organizational skills could amplify your ability to execute complex solutions more efficiently.

Using Strengths to Stand Out In today's competitive job market, standing out is essential, and leveraging your strengths can give you that edge. Employers are always looking for individuals who bring unique value to the table, and your strengths are what make you distinct. Being able to clearly communicate your strengths to potential employers or clients sets you apart as someone who knows their worth and how to deliver results.

For instance, during job interviews or performance reviews, rather than simply stating that you're "good at your job," be specific about your strengths. You could say, "I excel at building strong client relationships, and I have a proven track record of increasing client retention by 20% in my previous role." Highlighting concrete examples of how your strengths have led to success will make a strong impression and show that you understand how to apply your skills in practical ways.

Beyond standing out to employers, leveraging your strengths can also help you build a professional brand. In today's digital world, having a clear professional identity is important. Whether through LinkedIn profiles, personal websites, or professional networks, showcasing your strengths and expertise helps you build a reputation in your field. As you continue to grow your brand around your strengths, you'll attract opportunities that align with your skills and interests.

Balancing Strengths and Weaknesses While it's essential to focus on your strengths, it's also important to recognize that no one is perfect. We all have areas where we are not as strong. However, the key is to focus on **complementing your weaknesses** rather than letting them hold you back. This might involve collaborating with others whose strengths balance your weaknesses or investing in skill development to improve in areas where you're less proficient.

For example, if you excel at big-picture thinking but struggle with detail-oriented tasks, you could partner with a colleague who has strong organizational skills. This way, you're both playing to your strengths and creating a more balanced, effective team. Alternatively, you could take a course or workshop to enhance your attention to detail, thereby turning a weakness into an opportunity for growth.

By understanding your strengths and how to balance them with your weaknesses, you can create a more holistic approach to career success. Ultimately, the goal is not to be perfect at everything but to leverage what you do best while continuously learning and growing.

Conclusion: Turning Strengths into Success Identifying and leveraging your strengths is a powerful strategy for achieving career success. When you focus on what you naturally do well, you unlock higher levels of performance, enjoyment, and fulfillment in your work. By aligning your career goals with your strengths, seeking opportunities that play to your abilities, and strategically balancing your weaknesses, you set yourself up for long-term success in a way that feels authentic and rewarding.

Aligning Your Values with Your Career

One of the most overlooked aspects of career success is ensuring that your work aligns with your core values. Your values are the principles and beliefs that guide your actions and decisions. When your career aligns with your values, you find greater meaning and fulfillment in your work. On the other hand, when your career conflicts with your values, even a job that looks successful on the surface can feel empty or draining.

Why Values Matter in Career Success Values are the foundation of who you are and how you live your life. They represent what's most important to you, such as integrity, creativity, achievement, or helping others. In your career, these values influence the type of work you do, the people you choose to work with, and the kind of impact you want to make in the world. If you're unaware of your values or if you ignore them, you may find yourself pursuing goals that don't truly satisfy you.

For example, someone who values creativity might feel stifled in a rigid, rule-bound corporate environment, while someone who values making a difference might feel unfulfilled working in a role that lacks purpose or social impact. The key to long-term career satisfaction is aligning your work with your values so that your job becomes more than just a paycheck—it becomes a reflection of what you care about most.

Identifying Your Core Values Before you can align your career with your values, you need to first identify what those values are. This process requires self-reflection. Start by asking yourself questions like:

- What motivates me to get up in the morning?
- What are the qualities I admire most in others?
- When do I feel most fulfilled and why?
- What are the non-negotiables in my life?

These questions help you dig deep into what truly matters to you. Another useful exercise is to think about past experiences—both positive and negative—and reflect on how they made you feel. What aspects of those experiences resonated with your values, and which ones conflicted with them? For example, if you've felt most energized when collaborating with others and least satisfied when working in isolation, that might indicate that collaboration is a core value for you.

In addition to self-reflection, there are many values assessments available that can help you pinpoint your key values. These tools often present you with a list of values—such as autonomy, fairness, security, and adventure—and ask you to rank them in terms of importance. The goal is to identify your top five to ten values that are most meaningful to you.

The Impact of Values Misalignment When your career is not aligned with your values, it can lead to a host of problems, including stress, dissatisfaction, and burnout. You might feel like you're constantly compromising on what's important to you, which can create an inner tension. This tension can affect your motivation, productivity, and overall happiness.

For example, imagine you value work-life balance but find yourself in a demanding role that requires long hours and constant availability. Over time, the mismatch between your values and your job can lead to frustration, resentment, and even physical and emotional exhaustion. No matter how successful you are on paper, the misalignment between your values and your work will likely cause you to feel unfulfilled.

On the other hand, when your career aligns with your values, work feels more meaningful. You're more engaged, productive, and energized because you're not constantly fighting against what's important to you. You feel a sense of purpose and connection to your work, which not only enhances your performance but also contributes to your overall well-being.

Aligning Your Career with Your Values To align your career with your values, start by examining your current role and asking yourself whether it reflects what matters most to you. Are there aspects of your job that resonate with your values, and are there parts that feel out of sync? For example, if you value autonomy but find your job overly controlling, that could be a sign that your career is not fully aligned with your values.

If you discover areas of misalignment, don't panic. It's not always necessary to make a drastic career change. Sometimes, small adjustments can make a big difference. For example, if you value learning and growth but feel stagnant in your current position, you might seek out new training opportunities, take on projects that challenge you, or request a role with more responsibility. These changes can help bring your work more in line with your values without requiring a complete career overhaul.

However, if the gap between your values and your job is too wide to bridge, it may be time to consider a more significant career shift. This might mean exploring new industries, roles, or even entrepreneurship. For example, if you value creativity and freedom but feel trapped in a highly structured corporate environment, you might consider pursuing a role in a more innovative company or starting your own business. The key is to ensure that your next step brings you closer to work that aligns with your core values.

Living Your Values Every Day Once you've aligned your career with your values, the next step is to consciously live those values every day. It's not enough to simply work in a role that aligns with your principles—you need to actively embody those values in how you approach your work. This means making decisions that are consistent with your values, even when it's challenging.

For example, if you value integrity, you might face situations where you need to speak up against unethical practices, even if it's uncomfortable. If you value work-life balance, you might need to set boundaries with your employer or clients to protect your time. Living your values daily requires courage and commitment, but it also brings deep satisfaction because you're staying true to yourself.

Living your values at work not only brings personal fulfillment but also inspires others. When you lead by example and make decisions based on your principles, you become a role model for those around you. Whether you're leading a team or contributing as an individual, your actions can have a positive impact on your workplace culture, encouraging others to act with integrity and purpose.

Conclusion: Building a Values-Driven Career Aligning your career with your values is one of the most powerful ways to achieve long-term success and fulfillment. When your work reflects what matters most to you, it becomes a source of meaning and satisfaction, rather than just a means to an end. By identifying your core values, assessing whether your current role aligns with those values, and making adjustments as needed, you can create a career that feels authentic and deeply rewarding. Living your values every day allows you to stay connected to your purpose, bringing both personal and professional growth into harmony.

Defining Success on Your Own Terms

The traditional definitions of success—climbing the corporate ladder, earning a high salary, or achieving a prestigious title—don't necessarily reflect what success looks like for everyone. True success is deeply personal, and it means something different for each individual. It's not just about reaching a specific goal or milestone but about creating a life that aligns with your unique values, passions, and vision for the future. To experience genuine fulfillment in your career, you must define success on your own terms.

Why Traditional Success May Not Be Right for You

We live in a society where certain markers of success—money, power, status—are often emphasized as universal goals. From an early age, we're taught that a successful career involves climbing to the top of an organization, earning accolades, or building wealth. While these are certainly valid goals for some, they don't necessarily align with what everyone truly wants out of life.

For instance, a person might achieve a high-ranking position in a large company, but if that job requires sacrificing personal time, health, or meaningful relationships, they may feel unfulfilled despite their outward success. Similarly, someone who achieves financial wealth might feel empty if their work lacks purpose or passion.

It's important to recognize that success is not one-size-fits-all. What makes you feel successful might be entirely different from someone else's idea of achievement. This is why defining success on your own terms is crucial. If you're constantly chasing society's version of success, you may find yourself feeling dissatisfied, even when you've reached your goals.

What Does Success Mean to You?

To define success for yourself, start by asking a simple but powerful question: *What does success mean to me?* Think about the aspects of your life that bring you the most joy, satisfaction, and fulfillment. Is it having time for your family? Is it doing work that has a positive impact on others? Is it the freedom to travel or explore new ideas? Or is it mastering a skill or creative endeavor that you're passionate about?

Consider not just what success looks like in terms of outcomes, but how you want to feel along the way. Success is not only about achieving something significant—it's about enjoying the journey. Do you want to feel challenged, inspired, or balanced? Do you value autonomy and flexibility, or are structure and stability more important to you?

As you reflect on these questions, create a list of the qualities and experiences that define success for you. This list might include things like:

- *Freedom*: The ability to set your own schedule or pursue your passions.
- *Impact*: Making a difference in your community or in the lives of others.
- *Learning*: Continuously growing and expanding your skills and knowledge.
- *Balance*: Maintaining a healthy work-life balance that allows you to nurture relationships, health, and personal interests.
- *Fulfillment*: Doing work that feels meaningful and aligned with your purpose.

Defining success in these terms allows you to focus on what truly matters to you, rather than being swayed by external pressures or societal expectations.

Balancing Personal and Professional Success

One of the challenges in defining success on your own terms is balancing personal fulfillment with professional achievement. Many people feel torn between their personal goals—such as spending more time with loved ones or pursuing hobbies—and their professional aspirations. However, true success is about integrating both.

Instead of seeing your personal and professional lives as separate, consider how they can support each other. For example, if you value time with family, you might choose a career path that offers flexibility, allowing you to be present for important moments. If you're passionate about health and wellness, you might pursue a career in that field, so your professional work reflects your personal values.

Balancing these areas requires intention and self-awareness. It's about making choices that honor both your career goals and your desire for a fulfilling personal life. When you strike this balance, success becomes holistic—it's not just about professional accolades, but about living a well-rounded life that aligns with all of your values.

The Importance of Setting Boundaries

Defining success on your own terms also means setting boundaries that protect your vision of what success looks like. Once you know what's most important to you, it's essential to establish clear boundaries to ensure you don't get pulled off course by others' expectations or external demands.

For example, if you've defined success as maintaining a healthy work-life balance, you might need to set boundaries around your work hours, ensuring that you don't sacrifice family time for the sake of your career. If personal growth is part of your success definition, you might need to carve out time for activities like learning, meditation, or creative pursuits, even if it means saying no to other professional obligations.

Setting boundaries can be challenging, especially when it involves turning down opportunities or stepping back from roles that don't align with your vision. However, these boundaries are essential for staying true to your definition of success and avoiding burnout or resentment. Over time, setting boundaries helps you create a life that reflects your authentic goals, rather than constantly reacting to external pressures.

Redefining Success Over Time

Finally, it's important to remember that your definition of success may evolve over time. As you grow personally and professionally, your priorities and values may shift. What felt like success to you a decade ago may no longer resonate with where you are today.

For example, early in your career, you might have defined success as achieving financial security or gaining recognition in your field. But as your life circumstances change—perhaps with the addition of a family, new personal goals, or a desire for greater purpose—your definition of success may become more centered around balance, impact, or flexibility.

It's essential to periodically reflect on your definition of success and ask whether it still aligns with who you are and what you want out of life. If it doesn't, don't be afraid to adjust your goals and strategies. Success is a dynamic, ongoing journey, not a fixed destination.

Conclusion: Crafting Your Unique Path to Success

By defining success on your own terms, you take control of your career and your life. Instead of chasing someone else's version of success, you create a vision that reflects your values, passions, and goals. This approach allows you to experience greater fulfillment and purpose in your work, while also ensuring that your personal life remains balanced and meaningful.

Success, ultimately, is about living a life that feels authentic to you. It's about making decisions that honor your values, setting boundaries that protect your time and energy, and staying open to growth and change. When you define success for yourself, you empower yourself to create a life that's not just successful by external standards, but deeply rewarding on a personal level.

{ 7 }

Chapter 7: Enhancing Communication Skills

The Foundations of Effective Communication
Communication is the foundation of all human interaction. Whether you're engaging in a personal conversation, leading a business meeting, or writing an email, your ability to convey a message effectively can have a significant impact on the outcome of your interactions. Yet, effective communication is more than just speaking clearly—it's about ensuring that your message is understood as you intended and that you're also able to understand others. At its core, effective communication involves clarity, active listening, and empathy, all of which are essential for fostering meaningful connections.

Defining Effective Communication
Effective communication is often misunderstood as simply getting your point across. However, real communication is a two-way street. It requires not just the transmission of information, but also ensuring that the recipient fully understands that information. This means that communication doesn't just stop at speaking; it extends to how your message is received and interpreted.

To communicate effectively, clarity is key. You must be clear about what you want to say and ensure that your message is free from ambiguity. Whether you're giving instructions at work or sharing your thoughts with a friend, the clearer and more concise your message, the easier it will be for others to understand. Long-winded explanations, unnecessary jargon, or vague statements can lead to confusion and misunderstandings.

Equally important is being aware of your audience. Tailoring your communication to the person you're speaking with ensures that your message resonates with them. For example, speaking to a group of colleagues in a professional setting requires a different tone and vocabulary than a casual conversation with a friend. Effective communicators are adaptable, modifying their style based on the situation.

The Importance of Clarity and Conciseness

Clarity and conciseness go hand in hand in communication. Being clear means structuring your thoughts in a way that eliminates confusion, while being concise means delivering those thoughts in a way that is direct and to the point, without unnecessary details. These qualities are especially important in today's fast-paced world, where people often have limited attention spans.

Imagine trying to explain a complex idea in a meeting, but you end up rambling without making your key points clear. Your audience is likely to lose focus or misinterpret what you're saying. Conversely, if you can summarize your ideas in a clear and concise manner, people will not only understand your message but are more likely to remember and act on it.

One way to ensure clarity is by breaking down your message into simple, digestible parts. Instead of delivering a monologue, try to focus on one key idea at a time. This allows your listener to absorb the information fully before moving on to the next point. Additionally, ask yourself whether each part of your message is necessary—eliminate anything that doesn't directly support your main point.

Empathy in Communication

Effective communication is not just about delivering a message, but also about being able to understand the emotions, needs, and perspectives of others. This is where empathy plays a vital role. Empathy involves placing yourself in the other person's shoes and trying to see the world from their perspective. When you approach conversations with empathy, you become more attuned to the feelings and concerns of the person you're speaking to, which can help you communicate in a way that resonates with them.

For example, when giving feedback to a colleague, empathy allows you to frame your feedback in a way that acknowledges their efforts and encourages growth, rather than making them feel criticized. By demonstrating that you understand their point of view, you create a more supportive environment where open, honest communication can thrive.

Empathy also enhances your ability to listen. When you actively listen to someone with empathy, you don't just hear their words—you pay attention to their tone, body language, and the emotions behind what they're saying. This deeper understanding helps you respond in a way that validates their feelings and builds trust.

Avoiding Common Communication Pitfalls

Even the best communicators can fall into common traps that hinder effective communication. One such pitfall is making assumptions. We often assume that others know what we mean or that they share the same understanding of a topic. This can lead to miscommunication. To avoid this, it's important to regularly check in with the person you're speaking to. Ask questions to ensure they understand, and be open to clarifying your message if needed.

Another common pitfall is allowing distractions to interfere with communication. In today's digital age, distractions are everywhere. It's easy to become distracted by your phone, laptop, or even wandering thoughts during a conversation. However, effective communication requires full attention. When you're distracted, you may miss important details or unintentionally signal to the other person that their message isn't important to you.

A related issue is multitasking while communicating. Whether you're typing an email during a meeting or checking your phone while having a conversation, multitasking sends the message that the person you're speaking to doesn't have your full attention. It also limits your ability to truly engage with the other person, which can harm the quality of your communication.

Conclusion: Building a Strong Foundation

Effective communication begins with a strong foundation of clarity, active listening, and empathy. By focusing on these elements, you can ensure that your messages are understood and that you're able to understand others in return. Whether you're communicating with colleagues, friends, or family members, mastering these fundamentals will allow you to build stronger relationships, avoid misunderstandings, and achieve better outcomes in your personal and professional life. Communication isn't just about what you say—it's about how you make others feel, and how well you understand each other.

Active Listening and Its Impact on Relationships

Listening is one of the most important skills you can develop to elevate both your personal and professional life. Yet, it's also one of the most underrated. Most people think of communication as a primarily verbal act, focused on speaking clearly and articulating thoughts. But the truth is, effective communication relies just as much—if not more—on the ability to listen actively. Active listening transforms relationships, deepens understanding, and creates stronger connections. In this section, we'll explore what active listening really is, why it matters, and how you can develop this critical skill.

What Is Active Listening?

Active listening is more than simply hearing the words someone is saying. It's about fully engaging with the speaker, giving them your undivided attention, and making a conscious effort to understand their message. When you actively listen, you're not just waiting for your turn to speak. Instead, you're focused on the person in front of you, seeking to comprehend their perspective, emotions, and intentions.

Active listening involves several key elements:

- **Attention**: Giving the speaker your full focus, without distractions.
- **Reflection**: Summarizing or paraphrasing what the speaker has said to ensure you've understood correctly.
- **Feedback**: Responding appropriately to show that you're engaged and that you value their input.
- **Non-verbal Cues**: Maintaining eye contact, nodding, and using facial expressions that indicate you're paying attention.

These components work together to create a dialogue where both parties feel heard and understood. When people know that you're genuinely listening, they are more likely to open up, be honest, and engage in meaningful conversation.

Techniques for Becoming an Active Listener

Developing active listening skills requires practice and mindfulness. It's easy to fall into the habit of half-listening while thinking about what you're going to say next or allowing distractions to pull your attention away. However, by applying a few simple techniques, you can train yourself to become a more effective listener.

1. **Give Your Full Attention**: The first and most critical step in active listening is to be fully present. This means putting away distractions like your phone or laptop and focusing solely on the person speaking. If you're in a meeting, close any open tabs or documents that might steal your attention. When you make the speaker the center of your focus, you show them that what they're saying matters to you.

2. **Listen Without Interrupting**: It's tempting to jump in and offer your thoughts before the speaker has finished, but this can interrupt their flow and make them feel unheard. Let them complete their thoughts before you respond. This not only shows respect but also gives you the full context of their message.

3. **Paraphrase to Ensure Understanding**: After someone has spoken, one of the best ways to show that you've been listening is to paraphrase what they've said. For example, you might say, "So what I'm hearing is that you're concerned about the project's timeline. Is that correct?" This technique not only clarifies any potential misunderstandings but also reassures the speaker that you're engaged.

4. **Ask Open-Ended Questions**: Rather than responding with yes or no questions, ask open-ended questions that encourage the speaker to elaborate. This shows that you're interested in learning more and deepening your understanding of their perspective. For example, instead of asking, "Do you think the meeting went well?" try asking, "How do you feel about the meeting's outcome?"

5. **Practice Empathy**: Active listening requires more than just understanding the words being spoken; it also involves recognizing and acknowledging the emotions behind those words. If someone is sharing a frustration, for instance, acknowledge their feelings by saying, "I can see how that situation must have been really frustrating for you." Empathy fosters trust and strengthens relationships because it shows the other person that you care about their emotional experience.

How Active Listening Fosters Deeper Connections

Active listening has the power to transform relationships. Whether in the workplace, with friends, or in personal relationships, people who feel heard are more likely to trust and connect with you on a deeper level. This is because listening makes people feel valued. When you listen actively, you're showing the speaker that their thoughts, feelings, and experiences matter.

In a professional setting, active listening can help you become a better leader and team member. Leaders who practice active listening are more attuned to their team's needs, challenges, and ideas. Employees who feel heard are more engaged and motivated because they know their opinions count. Moreover, active listening can prevent misunderstandings that lead to workplace conflicts. By listening attentively, you can catch potential issues before they escalate, allowing for smoother collaboration and more effective problem-solving.

In personal relationships, active listening deepens emotional bonds. It allows you to understand your loved ones on a more profound level, strengthening trust and intimacy. When someone feels truly heard, they are more likely to share openly, creating a space for honest communication and mutual support.

Resolving Conflicts Through Active Listening

One of the most powerful applications of active listening is in conflict resolution. When tensions are high, people often listen only to respond rather than to understand. This can lead to miscommunication, frustration, and escalation. However, by employing active listening techniques, you can defuse conflicts and find common ground.

During a disagreement, actively listening to the other person's perspective helps you see the situation from their point of view. Even if you don't agree with them, acknowledging their feelings and concerns can soften the emotional intensity of the conflict. For instance, saying, "I understand that you feel upset about the missed deadline," shows that you're not dismissing their feelings, even if the reason for the missed deadline was beyond your control.

By practicing active listening in moments of conflict, you open the door to compromise and collaboration. The other person is more likely to reciprocate your listening efforts, creating a constructive dialogue where both parties can express their views and work toward a resolution.

Conclusion: Active Listening as a Path to Stronger Relationships

Active listening is a powerful tool that enhances every aspect of communication. It builds trust, strengthens connections, and fosters understanding. In a world where distractions are constant and time is often limited, taking the time to truly listen sets you apart. Whether you're at work or with loved ones, mastering the art of active listening will enrich your relationships and help you navigate difficult conversations with ease.

Listening is more than hearing words—it's about engaging with the speaker on a deeper level, understanding their thoughts, feelings, and intentions. By practicing active listening, you'll not only become a better communicator but also create an environment where others feel valued, respected, and understood.

The Art of Non-Verbal Communication

Communication isn't just about the words you speak. In fact, research shows that a significant portion of communication—up to 93%—is non-verbal. This includes your body language, facial expressions, gestures, posture, and even the tone of your voice. Often, the message you convey through your non-verbal cues can either reinforce or contradict the words coming out of your mouth. Understanding and mastering the art of non-verbal communication can significantly elevate your personal and professional relationships.

Why Non-Verbal Communication Matters

Non-verbal communication plays a crucial role in how others perceive you and how your message is received. Imagine walking into a meeting with slouched shoulders, avoiding eye contact, and speaking in a monotone voice. Even if your words are insightful, the lack of energy and confidence in your non-verbal cues will likely undermine the message you're trying to convey. On the other hand, maintaining eye contact, having an open posture, and speaking with enthusiasm will enhance the impact of your communication, helping you come across as credible, engaged, and confident.

Non-verbal cues can either strengthen or weaken your verbal communication. When your non-verbal signals align with your words, you create a sense of trust and clarity. For instance, if you're giving someone encouragement, a genuine smile or a supportive touch on the shoulder can reinforce your message. Conversely, if your non-verbal cues are inconsistent with what you're saying—such as offering praise while frowning or crossing your arms—it can cause confusion or mistrust.

Understanding the importance of non-verbal communication can help you become more aware of the signals you're sending to others. By consciously aligning your body language, facial expressions, and tone with your words, you can communicate more effectively and authentically.

Reading Others' Non-Verbal Cues

Just as your non-verbal communication is crucial to how others perceive you, learning to read the non-verbal cues of those around you is equally important. People often express their true feelings and thoughts through their body language, even if they don't say it out loud. Being attuned to these subtle cues can give you valuable insights into what someone is really thinking or feeling, helping you respond more empathetically.

For example, if you're in a conversation and the other person begins to fidget, cross their arms, or glance away frequently, these could be signs that they're uncomfortable or disengaged. On the other hand, leaning in, maintaining eye contact, and nodding along can indicate that they are interested and engaged in the conversation. Recognizing these signals allows you to adjust your approach and communication style in real time, making your interactions more dynamic and responsive.

Non-verbal cues are also crucial during conflict or tense situations. People may say they're fine or that nothing is wrong, but their body language can tell a different story. Paying attention to these signs can help you address underlying issues before they escalate.

Mastering Positive Body Language

Positive body language is essential for building rapport, trust, and effective communication. Whether you're leading a team, negotiating a deal, or simply having a conversation with a friend, your non-verbal communication speaks volumes. Here are a few key elements of positive body language that can help enhance your interactions:

1. **Maintain Eye Contact**: Eye contact is one of the most powerful tools in non-verbal communication. It shows that you're paying attention and that you're interested in the conversation. People who maintain appropriate eye contact are often perceived as more trustworthy and confident. However, be mindful of cultural differences and personal boundaries, as too much eye contact can sometimes be intimidating.

2. **Use Open Gestures**: Open gestures, such as uncrossed arms, an upright posture, and using your hands while speaking, signal openness and approachability. Crossing your arms or turning your body away from the speaker can give the impression that you're closed off or uninterested.

3. **Smile Authentically**: A genuine smile can go a long way in creating a positive connection. Smiling naturally releases tension, makes you appear more approachable, and can even make the person you're speaking with feel more at ease. However, it's important to be authentic—forced smiles can often be detected and may come across as insincere.

4. **Mirror the Other Person's Body Language**: Mirroring is a powerful technique in non-verbal communication. When you subtly mimic the other person's posture, gestures, or facial expressions, it helps create a sense of connection and rapport. This doesn't mean copying them exactly, but rather reflecting their energy and engagement in a way that feels natural.

5. **Be Mindful of Your Tone of Voice**: While your body language is important, the way you speak—the tone, pitch, and speed of your voice—also sends strong non-verbal signals. A calm, steady tone conveys confidence and clarity, while a shaky or rushed tone can indicate nervousness or uncertainty. Be mindful of how your voice can either reinforce or detract from the message you're trying to communicate.

The Role of Non-Verbal Communication in Professional Settings

In the workplace, non-verbal communication can be the difference between being perceived as a confident leader or a disengaged participant. For instance, if you're giving a presentation, how you stand, move, and gesture can greatly affect how your message is received. Standing tall with your shoulders back and making purposeful hand gestures can help you command the room and hold the audience's attention. On the other hand, slouching, avoiding eye contact, or pacing nervously can detract from your message and make you appear less credible.

In one-on-one conversations, non-verbal communication is just as crucial. Imagine you're having a difficult conversation with a colleague or client. If your body language is closed off—arms crossed, leaning back in your chair, or avoiding eye contact—it may signal that you're disinterested or defensive, even if your words say otherwise. Conversely, leaning in, maintaining eye contact, and keeping an open posture can help create an environment of trust and collaboration.

In leadership, your non-verbal communication sets the tone for your team. Employees often look to their leaders for cues on how to behave and what to expect. By demonstrating positive body language and non-verbal engagement, you not only enhance your own communication but also model the behaviors you want to see in your team.

Improving Your Non-Verbal Communication Skills

Improving your non-verbal communication requires self-awareness and practice. The first step is to become more conscious of your own body language and the non-verbal signals you're sending. Pay attention to how you stand, how you use your hands, and whether your facial expressions align with your words.

It's also helpful to get feedback from others. Ask trusted colleagues, friends, or mentors to observe your body language during meetings or conversations. They may notice things you hadn't considered—such as fidgeting, slouching, or lack of eye contact—that could be undermining your communication.

Finally, practice makes perfect. Try experimenting with different non-verbal techniques in low-stakes situations, such as casual conversations or team meetings. The more you practice positive body language, the more natural it will become.

Conclusion: Harnessing the Power of Non-Verbal Communication

Non-verbal communication is a powerful tool that can elevate your interactions, build stronger relationships, and enhance your professional presence. By mastering the art of body language, facial expressions, and tone, you can create deeper connections, inspire trust, and communicate more effectively. The next time you engage in a conversation—whether personal or professional—remember that what you're saying is only part of the story. Your body and actions speak just as loudly, if not louder, than your words.

Active Listening—The Key to Genuine Communication

Active listening is one of the most underrated, yet powerful, skills you can develop in your communication toolkit. While it may seem simple in theory, true active listening is much more than just hearing the words someone says. It involves fully engaging with the speaker, understanding their message, and responding thoughtfully. In both personal and professional interactions, mastering this skill can transform how you connect with others, leading to deeper relationships, greater trust, and improved outcomes.

The Difference Between Hearing and Listening

There's a big difference between hearing and listening. Hearing is a passive action—simply the physiological process of sound waves hitting your eardrums. You can hear someone without actually processing or understanding what they're saying. Listening, on the other hand, is an active and intentional process. It requires focus, concentration, and the ability to set aside your own thoughts and distractions in order to fully engage with the speaker.

Most of us fall into the trap of "hearing" instead of "listening" more often than we realize. How many times have you been in a conversation but found yourself mentally preparing your response while the other person was still talking? Or perhaps you've nodded along absentmindedly while your mind was elsewhere. These habits can be damaging, not only because they hinder your ability to fully understand the speaker's message but also because they signal disengagement.

Active listening is about being present in the moment. It means setting aside your internal dialogue and genuinely focusing on the other person. It's about giving them your full attention and making them feel heard and valued.

The Benefits of Active Listening

Active listening offers numerous benefits, both in your personal relationships and in your professional life. One of the most immediate advantages is that it fosters stronger connections. When someone feels genuinely listened to, they're more likely to trust you and open up. This builds rapport, deepens relationships, and creates a positive cycle of communication.

In professional settings, active listening can also enhance teamwork and collaboration. When team members feel that their opinions are valued and taken seriously, they're more likely to contribute meaningfully. This can lead to better decision-making, more innovative solutions, and a stronger sense of camaraderie within the team. Leaders who practice active listening are often seen as more empathetic, approachable, and trustworthy, which can greatly improve workplace dynamics.

Furthermore, active listening can help you avoid misunderstandings and conflicts. By taking the time to fully understand someone's point of view before responding, you reduce the risk of miscommunication. This is especially important in emotionally charged conversations, where misunderstandings can easily escalate into conflict. Active listening allows you to clarify issues early on, ensuring that both parties are on the same page.

How to Practice Active Listening

Developing your active listening skills requires mindfulness and practice. Here are some key strategies that can help you become a better listener:

1. **Give Your Full Attention**: This is the cornerstone of active listening. When someone is speaking, eliminate distractions and focus entirely on them. Put down your phone, close your laptop, and make a conscious effort to be present. This may sound simple, but in our constantly connected world, it's easy to get distracted. By giving the speaker your undivided attention, you show respect and signal that you value their input.

2. **Use Verbal and Non-Verbal Cues**: Engaging with the speaker through verbal and non-verbal cues lets them know you're actively listening. Simple gestures like nodding, maintaining eye contact, and saying things like "I see," "Go on," or "That makes sense" can encourage the speaker to continue sharing and confirm that you're following along. These cues demonstrate that you're not just hearing their words but also processing the information.

3. **Don't Interrupt**: One of the most common barriers to active listening is the temptation to interrupt. When someone is speaking, we often feel the urge to jump in with our own thoughts, opinions, or solutions. However, interrupting can derail the conversation and make the other person feel unheard. Practice holding back your responses until the speaker has finished. This gives them the space to fully express their thoughts and helps you avoid premature judgments or assumptions.

4. **Ask Clarifying Questions**: Active listening isn't about passively absorbing information; it's about engaging with the

speaker. Asking clarifying questions is a great way to show that you're genuinely interested in understanding their message. For example, if someone shares a complex idea, you might ask, "Can you elaborate on that?" or "What do you mean by...?" These types of questions not only help you gain a deeper understanding but also encourage the speaker to provide more context or detail.

5. **Paraphrase and Reflect**: One of the most effective techniques in active listening is paraphrasing what the speaker has said and reflecting it back to them. For instance, if a colleague explains a problem they're facing, you might respond with, "So, what I'm hearing is that you're frustrated with the lack of communication on the team. Is that correct?" This technique accomplishes two things: it confirms that you've understood their message, and it gives the speaker an opportunity to correct any misunderstandings. Paraphrasing also reinforces that you're paying attention and taking their concerns seriously.

The Impact of Active Listening on Relationships

When practiced consistently, active listening can have a transformative effect on your relationships. In personal interactions, it strengthens emotional bonds by fostering trust and mutual understanding. Partners, friends, and family members who feel heard are more likely to communicate openly and honestly, creating a more supportive and harmonious environment.

In professional relationships, active listening can enhance your reputation as a thoughtful and empathetic communicator. Whether you're managing a team, collaborating with colleagues, or negotiating with clients, the ability to listen actively can help you build credibility and influence. People are more inclined to follow your lead or support your ideas when they feel that their voices have been acknowledged and considered.

Active listening is also a powerful tool for conflict resolution. When disagreements arise, emotions often run high, and it's easy to become defensive or dismissive. However, by listening actively to the other person's perspective—without judgment or interruption—you can de-escalate tension and pave the way for constructive dialogue. This approach not only helps resolve conflicts more efficiently but also strengthens the relationship in the long run.

Conclusion: Elevating Communication Through Active Listening

Active listening is more than just a communication skill—it's a mindset. It requires a commitment to being present, empathetic, and open to truly understanding others. In a world where many people feel rushed or overlooked, mastering active listening can set you apart as a communicator who values connection and collaboration. Whether in your personal life or professional career, the ability to listen deeply and respond thoughtfully is a powerful asset that will elevate your relationships and interactions.

Communicating with Clarity—The Power of Precision

Communicating with clarity is a vital component of successful interactions, whether you're delivering a presentation at work, having a conversation with a friend, or writing an email. Clear communication ensures that your message is understood the way you intend, minimizing misunderstandings and confusion. In today's fast-paced world, where people are often juggling multiple priorities, clarity can be the difference between a productive exchange and a frustrating misunderstanding.

Why Clarity Matters

We've all experienced moments when communication has gone awry—where we thought we were being clear, but the other person misunderstood our message. Sometimes, we speak or write in a hurry, assuming the recipient understands the context or meaning behind our words. However, what's obvious to us may not be obvious to someone else, leading to confusion and misinterpretation.

Clarity in communication is crucial because it reduces ambiguity. It ensures that the person on the receiving end doesn't have to guess what you mean. In a professional setting, unclear instructions can lead to mistakes, missed deadlines, and inefficiency. In personal relationships, vague or poorly expressed emotions can lead to unnecessary conflict. By communicating clearly, you not only make sure your message is understood but also foster trust and respect with others.

How to Communicate Clearly

1. **Know Your Purpose**: Before speaking or writing, take a moment to think about the purpose of your message. What do you want to achieve from the conversation or communication? Is it to inform, persuade, or ask for something? Having a clear understanding of your objective helps you stay focused and avoid rambling. It ensures that everything you say contributes to that goal and prevents the conversation from going off-topic.

2. **Be Direct and Concise**: Being clear often means being concise. Don't use five words when one will do. Avoid jargon or overly complicated language, especially if you're speaking to someone who may not be familiar with the terms you're using. Simplicity is key to clarity. When you're direct and to the point, your message becomes easier to follow. This doesn't mean being abrupt or dismissive; it simply means

communicating in a way that's easy for the other person to understand.

3. **Organize Your Thoughts**: A well-organized message is much easier to understand than one that's disjointed. If you're speaking, structure your thoughts logically, and present them in a coherent order. Start with your main point, and then provide any necessary context or details. If you're writing, organize your message into clear sections or bullet points to make it easy to follow. This helps the recipient process the information without getting lost in a flood of unconnected ideas.

4. **Eliminate Assumptions**: One of the most common reasons for unclear communication is making assumptions about what the other person knows. We often assume that others have the same knowledge, context, or perspective that we do. However, this can lead to miscommunication, especially if the other person lacks important information. Instead, take the time to explain any necessary background or context to ensure that the recipient fully understands your message. If you're unsure about their level of understanding, ask questions to gauge their knowledge.

5. **Clarify and Confirm**: After you've communicated your message, it's important to confirm that the other person has understood it correctly. This is particularly crucial in situations where the details are important, such as giving instructions for a project or discussing sensitive topics in a relationship. You can ask the other person to repeat back what they've heard or understood, or you can check in by asking, "Does that make sense?" or "Is there anything I need to clarify?"

The Role of Feedback in Clarity

Feedback is a powerful tool for improving clarity in communication. Whether you're giving or receiving feedback, it helps ensure that both parties are on the same page. When giving feedback, be clear and specific about what worked and what could be improved. This avoids vague generalities that might leave the other person uncertain about what you're asking of them.

Similarly, when receiving feedback, encourage the other person to be specific about what they understood. If they express confusion or misunderstand something, use it as an opportunity to clarify your message further. Open dialogue and a willingness to adjust your communication approach can dramatically improve clarity over time.

In professional environments, feedback is especially important when dealing with teams or clients. A clear and well-communicated project plan, for example, should be followed up with feedback from team members to ensure everyone understands their roles and responsibilities. This not only improves efficiency but also reduces the likelihood of errors.

Non-Verbal Communication and Clarity

While words are critical for clear communication, non-verbal cues play an equally important role. Body language, facial expressions, and tone of voice all contribute to how your message is perceived. Sometimes, our words may be clear, but our body language sends a different signal, creating confusion.

For example, if you're telling someone that you're happy with their work but your tone sounds disinterested or your body language appears closed off, the recipient may interpret your message as insincere. Ensuring that your non-verbal communication aligns with your words is key to maintaining clarity.

One effective way to manage this is through conscious aware-ness of your non-verbal signals. When you're speaking, ensure your body language is open, maintain eye contact, and use ges-tures that reinforce your message. A warm and encouraging tone can also enhance the clarity of your message, especially in situa-tions where emotions are involved.

The Benefits of Clear Communication

Clear communication has a profound impact on all areas of life. In professional settings, it increases productivity, reduces er-rors, and fosters better collaboration. When team members com-municate clearly with one another, they're more likely to achieve their goals and work together harmoniously. Leaders who com-municate with clarity are often more respected and trusted, as their team members know what is expected of them and can rely on transparent guidance.

In personal relationships, clear communication builds trust and intimacy. It allows you to express your feelings and needs without the fear of being misunderstood, creating a foundation for strong and healthy relationships. When people feel that they can communicate openly and clearly with one another, it deepens emotional connections and prevents unnecessary conflict.

Conclusion: The Path to Clear Communication

Communicating with clarity is not about being perfect or al-ways getting it right the first time. It's about being mindful of your words, ensuring your message is understood, and being will-ing to clarify when necessary. By focusing on clear, concise, and direct communication, you empower yourself and those around you to engage in meaningful, productive conversations. Whether in personal interactions or professional environments, clear com-munication will elevate your relationships, improve efficiency, and build a foundation of trust and understanding.

{ **8** }

Chapter 8: Building Leadership Abilities

Understanding the Essence of Leadership

Leadership is a term that's often thrown around in the corporate world, but its true essence goes far beyond job titles and executive positions. At its core, leadership is about influence—specifically, the ability to inspire, guide, and motivate others toward a shared vision or goal. Whether you're a CEO, a team leader, or someone without a formal leadership role, understanding the true essence of leadership can empower you to lead effectively in any situation.

The first thing to understand is that **leadership and management are not the same**. Management is about overseeing processes, ensuring tasks are completed, and maintaining order. Leaders, on the other hand, inspire innovation, drive change, and push people toward a collective goal. While effective leaders need management skills, and vice versa, true leadership is more about influence than authority. A leader's role is to inspire others to follow—not because they have to, but because they want to.

One of the greatest misconceptions about leadership is that it's tied to a position. People often assume that only those in senior roles are "leaders," but that's simply not the case. Leadership can occur at any level of an organization or in any aspect of life. You don't need a title to lead; you only need the desire and willingness to influence those around you positively. Think of those individuals who naturally command respect and motivate others without being in formal leadership positions. These people embody the essence of leadership, showing that influence is about actions and mindset, not titles.

Vision and Purpose: The Cornerstones of Leadership

At the heart of effective leadership is **vision**. Leaders see possibilities and opportunities that others may overlook. They look beyond the immediate challenges and circumstances to create a long-term vision that excites and motivates people. However, having a vision isn't enough. Leaders must be able to communicate this vision in a way that resonates with their team or followers. A compelling vision isn't just a grand idea—it connects with the people involved, giving them a sense of purpose and direction.

Consider leaders like **Martin Luther King Jr.** or **Steve Jobs**—both had compelling visions. King's vision for a society of equality and Jobs' vision for groundbreaking technology weren't just personal aspirations; they were ideas that inspired millions. These leaders had the ability to communicate their visions so clearly that others could see them, feel them, and want to be a part of them. This is one of the core aspects of leadership: providing a vision that aligns with the values and desires of those you seek to lead.

The Importance of Influence

Influence is another key element that defines leadership. But influence doesn't come from authority; it comes from earning trust, respect, and credibility over time. True leaders influence others through their actions, words, and ability to connect on a human level. They listen, they empathize, and they lead by example. Influence allows a leader to guide others without force or manipulation, creating a team environment where people want to contribute and give their best.

One of the ways leaders build influence is through **empathy and active listening**. By understanding the needs and perspectives of others, leaders can tailor their communication and approach to resonate with their team or followers. This is how influence is nurtured—through connection, trust, and mutual respect.

A great leader also understands that influence is a two-way street. While they guide and motivate others, they also allow themselves to be influenced by the insights and contributions of their team. They aren't rigid in their approach but are open to learning and adapting.

Leadership is a Skill, Not a Trait

Another key point to understand is that leadership is not an innate trait reserved for a select few. It is a **learned skill** that anyone can develop over time. While some people may naturally exhibit certain qualities associated with leadership, like charisma or decisiveness, these qualities alone do not make someone a leader. Leadership requires continuous self-improvement, learning, and development. The most effective leaders are those who are constantly seeking to grow—not just for their own benefit, but to better serve and support those they lead.

In fact, some of the greatest leaders in history didn't start off as natural-born leaders. They grew into their roles through experience, mistakes, and a commitment to learning. Leadership development is a lifelong journey, one that involves mastering new skills, cultivating self-awareness, and constantly seeking to elevate others.

Leadership in Everyday Life

While leadership is often associated with the workplace or large-scale movements, the reality is that **leadership exists in all areas of life**. You can be a leader in your family, your community, or your social circles. Leadership doesn't require a title; it requires action. It's about stepping up when others need guidance, offering support when someone is struggling, and showing the way when others can't see the path forward.

In your daily life, opportunities to lead are everywhere. Whether you're mentoring a colleague, supporting a friend through a tough time, or volunteering in your community, leadership is about making a positive difference in the lives of others. These smaller acts of leadership are just as important as leading a team or organization because they build the foundation for greater influence and impact.

In summary, leadership is about far more than overseeing tasks or managing people. It's about influence, vision, and the ability to guide others toward a shared goal. Whether you're in a formal leadership role or simply looking to make a positive impact in your everyday life, understanding the essence of leadership is the first step toward becoming a leader who inspires, motivates, and elevates others. Leadership is not defined by titles, but by the willingness to step up, take responsibility, and influence others in meaningful ways.

Developing Emotional Intelligence

Emotional intelligence (EQ) is one of the most critical aspects of effective leadership. While intelligence and technical skills are essential in any professional or personal setting, emotional intelligence is what truly sets great leaders apart. Leaders with high emotional intelligence are able to navigate complex interpersonal dynamics, manage their own emotions effectively, and inspire trust and loyalty in those around them. Developing emotional intelligence is not just a key to becoming a better leader—it's essential for personal growth and relationship building in all areas of life.

Self-Awareness: The Foundation of Emotional Intelligence

At the heart of emotional intelligence is **self-awareness**—the ability to recognize and understand your own emotions, strengths, weaknesses, and how they impact your thoughts and behavior. Leaders who are self-aware can accurately assess their own emotional state and its effect on others. This awareness helps them avoid impulsive reactions, maintain control in challenging situations, and make better decisions.

Self-awareness also extends to understanding your core values and motivations. When you're clear about what drives you, it becomes easier to align your leadership style with your values. For example, if one of your core values is integrity, being self-aware will help you remain authentic and consistent in your leadership approach, even when faced with difficult decisions. Moreover, self-awareness allows you to recognize when your emotions are affecting your judgment or interactions with others, enabling you to adjust your behavior and remain calm and focused.

Developing self-awareness requires taking a step back to observe your emotions and behavior in various situations. Regular reflection, journaling, and even seeking feedback from others can help you cultivate greater awareness of your emotional patterns and how they influence your leadership.

Self-Regulation: Managing Emotions Effectively

Once you've developed self-awareness, the next step in building emotional intelligence is **self-regulation**—the ability to manage and control your emotions, particularly in stressful or high-pressure situations. Leaders who can regulate their emotions are able to stay calm and composed, even when faced with adversity or conflict. This level-headedness allows them to make more thoughtful decisions and prevents them from lashing out or reacting impulsively.

Self-regulation is not about suppressing your emotions, but rather managing them in a healthy way. It's about being able to pause, assess the situation, and choose a response that aligns with your long-term goals and values. For example, in a heated discussion, a leader with strong self-regulation will resist the urge to respond with anger or frustration. Instead, they will take a moment to breathe, listen, and respond in a way that de-escalates the situation and fosters constructive dialogue.

A key component of self-regulation is maintaining **emotional resilience**. Resilient leaders can handle setbacks, criticism, and challenges without being overwhelmed or discouraged. They remain focused on the bigger picture and use their emotional regulation skills to bounce back from adversity, setting an example for their team or peers.

Empathy: Understanding and Connecting with Others

Empathy, the ability to understand and share the feelings of others, is one of the most powerful tools in a leader's emotional intelligence toolkit. Leaders who are empathetic can tune into the emotions and concerns of their team members, colleagues, or clients, which enables them to build deeper, more meaningful relationships. Empathy is about recognizing and validating others' emotions, making them feel seen and heard.

In a leadership context, empathy plays a vital role in **effective communication** and **conflict resolution**. When leaders take the time to understand the perspectives and emotions of others, they are better equipped to address misunderstandings, resolve disagreements, and foster collaboration. For instance, if a team member is struggling with personal issues, an empathetic leader would recognize this and offer support or flexibility, rather than simply focusing on performance metrics.

Empathy also helps leaders navigate difficult conversations, such as delivering feedback or addressing underperformance. When leaders approach these discussions with empathy, they are more likely to frame their feedback in a way that is constructive and supportive, rather than punitive. This not only leads to better outcomes but also strengthens the trust and rapport between leaders and their teams.

Social Skills: Building Strong Relationships

Strong leadership requires the ability to build and maintain positive relationships with others, and this is where **social skills** come into play. Leaders with strong social skills are effective communicators, able to navigate complex group dynamics, and adept at fostering a collaborative, inclusive environment. Social skills encompass a range of abilities, including active listening, verbal and nonverbal communication, conflict management, and teamwork.

Leaders with high emotional intelligence know how to **connect with others** on a personal level, whether through one-on-one conversations or team interactions. They are skilled at reading social cues and understanding the unspoken dynamics of a group. For example, in a meeting, a leader with strong social skills can sense when someone feels left out of the conversation and will make an effort to include them, ensuring that all voices are heard.

Another critical aspect of social skills is **influence**. Leaders who build strong relationships based on trust and mutual respect are more likely to influence others positively. They can inspire collaboration, motivate their teams, and foster a culture of open communication, where everyone feels comfortable sharing their ideas and concerns.

Motivation: Leading with Purpose and Passion

The final component of emotional intelligence is **motivation**—the internal drive to achieve, grow, and inspire others to do the same. Emotionally intelligent leaders are deeply motivated by their passion for their work and their desire to make a positive impact. This intrinsic motivation not only fuels their own success but also inspires those around them.

Leaders who are motivated by more than just external rewards, like promotions or financial gain, are better equipped to weather challenges and setbacks. They have a sense of purpose that keeps them focused on their long-term goals, even when obstacles arise. Their passion and enthusiasm are contagious, helping to create a positive, energized work environment.

Moreover, motivated leaders are **committed to personal and professional growth**. They continually seek to improve themselves, learn new skills, and push their teams to reach higher levels of performance. By modeling this commitment to growth, emotionally intelligent leaders encourage others to strive for excellence and take ownership of their development.

In conclusion, developing emotional intelligence is crucial for anyone aspiring to lead effectively. By cultivating self-awareness, self-regulation, empathy, social skills, and motivation, leaders can navigate the complexities of human relationships with grace and wisdom, ultimately building stronger, more cohesive teams and creating lasting positive impact.

Cultivating a Growth Mindset

A fundamental trait that distinguishes successful leaders from others is their ability to cultivate a growth mindset. Coined by psychologist Carol Dweck, a growth mindset is the belief that abilities and intelligence can be developed through hard work, dedication, and learning from failures. In contrast to a fixed mindset, which views talent and intelligence as static, a growth mindset encourages continuous improvement and resilience in the face of challenges. For leaders, adopting this mindset is essential for not only their personal development but also for fostering a culture of innovation and improvement within their teams.

Embracing Challenges as Opportunities

Leaders with a growth mindset see challenges not as threats to their competence but as opportunities to grow. This perspective shift makes a tremendous difference in how they approach difficult situations. Instead of avoiding challenges or feeling overwhelmed, they confront them head-on, viewing each obstacle as a stepping stone toward mastery.

For example, imagine a leader tasked with a major organizational change, such as implementing a new technology system. While this might feel overwhelming, a leader with a growth mindset sees the opportunity to develop new skills, innovate solutions, and ultimately improve the organization. They understand that setbacks and difficulties are a natural part of the learning process, and they maintain a solution-oriented approach.

Cultivating this mindset requires reframing how you perceive difficulties. Rather than fearing failure, it involves seeing each challenge as a moment to learn something new. This proactive attitude not only boosts personal resilience but also sets a powerful example for others. Leaders who openly embrace challenges inspire their teams to take risks, innovate, and push boundaries, fostering a culture of growth.

Learning from Feedback and Failure

A growth mindset is rooted in the understanding that feedback and failure are integral to the learning process. Leaders who embrace this mindset actively seek feedback, not just when things go wrong but also to identify areas where they can improve. They recognize that no one achieves excellence without making mistakes along the way, and they see failure as an opportunity for reflection and growth.

One hallmark of a leader with a growth mindset is their willingness to **be vulnerable** and admit when they don't have all the answers. Rather than trying to project an image of infallibility, they show humility by acknowledging mistakes and actively seeking out ways to improve. This humility fosters trust and psychological safety within their team, creating an environment where everyone feels comfortable taking risks and learning from their own errors.

For example, when a project doesn't go as planned, a fixed-mindset leader might react defensively, placing blame or making excuses. A growth-minded leader, on the other hand, would take responsibility, analyze what went wrong, and use the experience as a valuable lesson. This reflective process allows them to continuously improve and adapt.

Encouraging Continuous Learning and Development

Leaders with a growth mindset are lifelong learners. They constantly seek new knowledge, whether through formal education, mentorship, or personal experiences. This commitment to learning isn't limited to areas where they already excel—it extends to those areas where they need the most growth. Whether it's developing better communication skills, improving technical knowledge, or mastering new leadership techniques, growth-minded leaders never stop evolving.

Moreover, leaders with a growth mindset actively encourage their teams to adopt the same approach to learning. They create an environment where **continuous development** is valued, providing resources for their team members to upskill, experiment, and expand their horizons. This could involve offering opportunities for professional development, encouraging team members to attend workshops, or simply fostering a culture where curiosity and learning are rewarded.

In a fast-changing world, this commitment to ongoing development is crucial. Industries evolve, technologies advance, and the expectations placed on leaders and teams shift. By fostering a growth mindset, leaders ensure that they and their teams stay adaptable, resilient, and ahead of the curve.

Viewing Effort as the Path to Mastery

Leaders with a growth mindset understand that effort is not only necessary for success but also the very thing that makes success meaningful. In a fixed mindset, people often believe that talent alone determines achievement. However, a growth-minded leader recognizes that while talent can provide a head start, consistent effort and perseverance are what truly lead to mastery.

This belief in the power of effort has profound implications for leadership. First, it helps leaders develop **grit**, the determination to keep going in the face of setbacks. They don't give up easily because they see hard work as an investment in their future success. They also understand that improvement comes gradually and that mastery requires patience and persistence.

Secondly, a focus on effort helps leaders maintain a sense of **personal accountability**. When things don't go as planned, they don't blame external factors or look for easy excuses. Instead, they ask themselves, "What could I have done differently?" This introspective approach allows them to learn from their experiences and adjust their strategies.

Finally, growth-minded leaders instill the value of hard work within their teams. They praise effort and perseverance, not just results. This creates a culture where people feel empowered to take risks, put in the necessary work, and ultimately achieve greater things. By emphasizing the importance of effort, leaders inspire their teams to push through obstacles and strive for continuous improvement.

Fostering a Culture of Innovation and Adaptability

A growth mindset is a catalyst for innovation. Leaders who believe in the potential for growth and improvement are more likely to encourage creative thinking, experimentation, and out-of-the-box solutions. They understand that innovation often involves trial and error, and they are willing to take calculated risks to push boundaries and explore new possibilities.

This mindset fosters an **environment of adaptability**—a crucial quality in today's fast-paced, ever-evolving world. Growth-minded leaders aren't afraid to change course when necessary, and they encourage their teams to remain agile and open to new ideas. By promoting a culture where learning from failure is valued and experimentation is encouraged, leaders create a fertile ground for innovation to flourish.

Moreover, a growth mindset enables leaders to be more flexible in the face of disruption. Whether it's adapting to new market trends, embracing new technologies, or navigating economic shifts, leaders who believe in the power of growth and adaptability are better equipped to lead their organizations through change.

In conclusion, cultivating a growth mindset is essential for anyone striving to become a better leader. By embracing challenges, learning from feedback and failure, encouraging continuous learning, valuing effort, and fostering innovation, leaders can elevate not only their own potential but also that of the teams and organizations they serve. A growth mindset is the key to unlocking resilience, adaptability, and long-term success in both personal and professional arenas.

Leading by Example

One of the most impactful ways a leader can inspire and elevate those around them is by leading through their own actions. Leadership is not merely about directing or delegating tasks—it's about embodying the values, work ethic, and attitude that you want to see in others. People are far more likely to follow a leader who demonstrates integrity, commitment, and resilience in their daily behavior. Leading by example builds trust, fosters respect, and sets the tone for the culture within a team or organization.

Modeling the Behaviors You Want to See

As a leader, your team is constantly observing your behavior, even in ways you might not realize. Whether it's how you handle stress, your response to setbacks, or how you treat others, your actions send a powerful message. If you want your team to be innovative, you must show that you are open to new ideas and willing to take calculated risks. If you want them to persevere in the face of challenges, you must demonstrate resilience and a solution-oriented mindset when things don't go as planned.

For instance, if a leader advocates for a healthy work-life balance but is constantly working late, sending emails at all hours, and burning out, the team receives mixed signals. They may feel pressured to mimic those behaviors to gain approval or recognition, leading to lower morale and productivity. On the other hand, when leaders model positive behaviors like time management, prioritizing well-being, and setting clear boundaries, they create an environment that supports the growth and well-being of the entire team.

The most effective leaders show by example that they practice what they preach. Their actions align with their words, fostering an atmosphere of accountability and trust. This consistency is crucial because when leaders act with integrity and purpose, their teams are more likely to respect and emulate those qualities.

Demonstrating Emotional Intelligence

A key part of leading by example is demonstrating emotional intelligence (EQ). Leaders who show empathy, self-awareness, and the ability to manage their emotions under pressure set a standard for how to navigate the complexities of the workplace. Emotional intelligence is often what separates a good leader from a great one because it involves understanding and managing not only your own emotions but also recognizing and responding to the emotions of others.

For example, in a stressful situation where a project is running behind schedule, a leader with high emotional intelligence will approach the problem with a calm and composed demeanor. Rather than reacting with frustration or panic, they will assess the situation, communicate clearly with the team, and focus on finding solutions. This calm, proactive response will help the team stay focused and motivated, even under pressure.

Moreover, leaders who demonstrate empathy create a work environment where people feel valued and understood. When team members face personal or professional challenges, leaders who show they genuinely care about their well-being help foster loyalty and motivation. By modeling emotional intelligence, leaders can cultivate a culture of trust, respect, and collaboration.

Showing Commitment to Continuous Growth

If you want your team to grow, you need to show that you are committed to your own growth as well. Leaders who embrace continuous learning and development set an example for their teams to follow. They demonstrate that no matter where you are in your career, there is always room to improve and evolve. This mindset creates a ripple effect, encouraging others to seek out opportunities for personal and professional growth.

For instance, a leader who attends workshops, takes courses, and engages in mentorship programs shows their team that learning is a lifelong process. This visible commitment to self-improvement inspires others to follow suit, creating a culture where everyone is striving to enhance their skills and knowledge. Moreover, leaders who actively seek feedback and work on their own development show that growth is a shared value within the team or organization.

By embracing vulnerability and acknowledging that they, too, have areas to improve, leaders foster a sense of psychological safety within the team. Team members feel more comfortable admitting mistakes, seeking help, and taking risks when they see their leader modeling those behaviors. This openness to growth is contagious, helping to elevate the performance of the entire team.

Building Trust and Accountability

Leading by example is one of the most effective ways to build trust. When leaders consistently act with integrity, make ethical decisions, and treat others with respect, they earn the trust of their team. Trust is the foundation of any successful team or organization because it fosters collaboration, open communication, and a shared sense of responsibility.

For example, if a leader expects accountability from their team members, they must first hold themselves accountable. This means owning up to mistakes, being transparent about decisions, and following through on commitments. When leaders demonstrate personal accountability, they encourage others to do the same. Teams that trust their leaders are more likely to take ownership of their work, be honest about challenges, and collaborate more effectively.

Furthermore, leading by example creates a culture where accountability is expected at all levels. Rather than focusing on blame when things go wrong, a leader who models accountability will guide the team to focus on solutions and learning from mistakes. This approach fosters a growth-oriented culture where people feel safe to take responsibility for their actions, ultimately leading to higher performance and better outcomes.

Creating a Positive and Motivational Culture

Leaders who lead by example have a profound influence on the overall culture of their team or organization. By consistently demonstrating the values of hard work, resilience, and collaboration, they create a positive and motivational environment. Team members are more likely to feel inspired and energized when they see their leader putting in the effort and maintaining a positive attitude, even in the face of adversity.

For example, a leader who remains optimistic and focused during challenging times can uplift the entire team. This positivity becomes infectious, helping to maintain high morale and motivation. On the other hand, leaders who complain, blame others, or give up when things get tough can quickly demoralize their teams. The culture a leader creates through their actions has a direct impact on the engagement, productivity, and success of the team.

In conclusion, leading by example is one of the most powerful tools a leader has. It involves modeling the behaviors, values, and attitudes that you want to see in others. By demonstrating integrity, emotional intelligence, commitment to growth, accountability, and positivity, leaders can inspire their teams to reach new heights. The example you set as a leader has a lasting impact, shaping the culture of your team and driving success in both personal and professional realms.

Empowering Others to Lead

True leadership is not about maintaining control or being the sole decision-maker. It's about empowering others to step into leadership roles themselves, fostering a culture where everyone feels capable of contributing and growing. By empowering others, a leader creates a ripple effect—developing new leaders, increasing team engagement, and driving better overall results. The best leaders understand that their role is not to hold power but to distribute it in ways that allow others to shine and make an impact.

Delegating with Trust and Confidence

One of the most critical aspects of empowering others is effective delegation. Many leaders struggle with letting go of control, fearing that tasks won't be done as well as they would do them themselves. However, delegation is not about passing off work but rather about entrusting others with meaningful responsibilities and providing them with the opportunity to grow.

When a leader delegates with trust, they signal to their team that they have confidence in their abilities. This builds a sense of ownership and accountability, motivating individuals to do their best work. It also helps people develop new skills and experience, fostering their professional growth. By delegating effectively, leaders create a dynamic team where people feel empowered to take initiative, make decisions, and contribute to the organization's success.

For instance, a leader might assign a high-visibility project to a junior team member, giving them the chance to step into a leadership role. By providing clear expectations, guidance, and feedback, the leader ensures that the individual has the support they need to succeed. At the same time, the team member gains valuable experience and confidence, which will serve them well in future roles.

Encouraging Autonomy and Innovation

Empowering others also means giving them the freedom to work autonomously and explore innovative solutions. Micromanagement stifles creativity and limits personal growth, while autonomy fosters a sense of ownership and encourages individuals to think critically and take initiative. Leaders who empower their teams to make decisions and explore new ideas are often rewarded with innovative solutions that drive progress.

To foster autonomy, leaders must trust their team members to make decisions and solve problems on their own. This doesn't mean abandoning oversight but rather creating a space where people feel safe to experiment, learn from failures, and come up with creative solutions. When leaders encourage innovation and allow for calculated risks, they create a culture of continuous improvement and forward-thinking.

For example, if a leader encourages their team to brainstorm and implement new strategies for improving workflow efficiency, they may uncover ideas that hadn't been considered before. By empowering the team to lead these initiatives, the leader not only fosters innovation but also helps the team develop a sense of ownership over the improvements they implement.

Providing Opportunities for Leadership Development

An essential part of empowering others to lead is providing them with opportunities to develop their leadership skills. This can be done through mentorship, training programs, or simply by giving individuals the chance to take on leadership roles within projects or teams. Leaders who actively invest in the development of their team members create a culture where growth is encouraged and leadership potential is nurtured.

Leaders can create opportunities for development by identifying team members with leadership potential and offering them roles that challenge their skills. This could involve assigning them to lead a small team on a project, manage a client relationship, or take on a critical decision-making role. By offering these opportunities, leaders give individuals the chance to practice and refine their leadership abilities in a supportive environment.

Moreover, providing regular feedback and guidance is crucial in this process. Leaders who offer constructive feedback help individuals grow and learn from their experiences, preparing them for larger leadership roles in the future. This approach not only empowers team members but also strengthens the overall leadership capacity of the organization.

Fostering a Collaborative Leadership Culture

Empowering others to lead doesn't just benefit the individual—it enhances the entire team dynamic. When leadership is distributed across a team, collaboration thrives, and the collective intelligence of the group increases. Leaders who foster a collaborative leadership culture create an environment where everyone feels empowered to contribute their ideas, challenge assumptions, and work together towards common goals.

In a collaborative leadership culture, the hierarchy becomes less rigid, and decision-making becomes more inclusive. Team members feel valued for their input and are more willing to take ownership of both successes and challenges. This leads to stronger collaboration, improved communication, and better problem-solving across the board.

A leader might encourage this culture by regularly hosting team meetings where everyone is encouraged to share their ideas and contribute to decision-making. By giving each person a voice, the leader shows that leadership is a shared responsibility, and everyone's input is valuable. This approach leads to a more engaged and motivated team that feels collectively responsible for achieving the organization's objectives.

Recognizing and Celebrating Leadership Contributions

Finally, empowering others to lead involves recognizing and celebrating their contributions. Acknowledging the efforts of team members who step into leadership roles not only reinforces their confidence but also motivates others to take on similar responsibilities. Recognition is a powerful tool for encouraging leadership at all levels and fostering a culture of empowerment.

Leaders can recognize contributions in many ways, from public praise in team meetings to more formal rewards or opportunities for advancement. Celebrating the successes of those who have taken on leadership roles shows the team that stepping up is valued and appreciated. It also reinforces the idea that leadership is not limited to a title but is defined by actions and contributions.

For example, if a team member successfully leads a project to completion, a leader might highlight their contributions in a team meeting, emphasizing how their leadership made a difference. This recognition not only boosts the individual's confidence but also encourages others to seek out leadership opportunities, knowing that their efforts will be acknowledged and appreciated.

In conclusion, empowering others to lead is a cornerstone of effective leadership. By delegating with trust, fostering autonomy, providing development opportunities, encouraging collaboration, and recognizing contributions, leaders create an environment where leadership is shared and growth is continuous. When leaders focus on empowering others, they build stronger teams, inspire innovation, and elevate the performance of everyone around them. This ripple effect of empowerment is the hallmark of a true leader.

{ **9** }

Chapter 9: Fostering Creativity and Innovation

Understanding the Foundations of Creativity

Creativity is often misunderstood. Many people assume that being creative is a rare, innate talent that only artists, musicians, or writers possess. However, this view limits the true scope of creativity. In reality, creativity is much broader and more accessible than most of us realize. It is not confined to artistic pursuits; instead, it is the ability to approach challenges and situations in new, original, and inventive ways. Whether you're solving a complex problem at work, coming up with a new idea for a business, or even rethinking how you organize your day, you're engaging in a creative process.

At its core, creativity is about thinking differently. It's about breaking free from traditional patterns of thought and exploring new possibilities. When we think creatively, we open ourselves up to new ways of seeing the world. This shift in perspective is what allows us to innovate, to find solutions where others see only obstacles, and to come up with ideas that are both fresh and valuable.

Creativity and Innovation: What's the Difference?

Before we dive deeper, it's important to clarify the distinction between creativity and innovation. While these terms are often used interchangeably, they are not the same. Creativity is the generation of new and original ideas, while innovation is the process of implementing those ideas to create something useful or beneficial. Think of creativity as the spark and innovation as the fire. Creativity is the brainstorming, the imagining, the free-flowing of ideas. Innovation is when those ideas take shape and lead to action, solving real-world problems or creating something new.

Understanding this distinction helps us appreciate that creativity is the essential first step in any process of innovation. Without the generation of ideas, there can be no innovation. But without action, creativity remains an untapped potential.

Debunking the Myths of Creativity

One of the biggest myths about creativity is that it's an innate trait—something you're either born with or you're not. This belief holds many people back from exploring their own creative potential. The truth is, everyone has the ability to be creative. Like any skill, creativity can be cultivated and developed over time.

Another common myth is that creativity only happens in sudden bursts of inspiration, often referred to as "eureka moments." While these moments do happen, they are often the result of sustained effort and exploration. Creativity is less about waiting for inspiration to strike and more about cultivating habits that allow you to think creatively on a regular basis. It's a process, not an event.

Finally, there's the misconception that creativity is only useful in certain fields. Many people believe that unless they're working in a traditionally creative industry, such as the arts or design, there's little need for creativity in their daily lives. This couldn't be further from the truth. Creativity is essential in every field, from business and technology to education and healthcare. Wherever there are problems to solve or improvements to be made, creativity is required.

The Role of Curiosity in Fostering Creativity

At the heart of creativity is curiosity. Curiosity is the driving force that pushes us to explore the unknown, to ask questions, and to seek out new knowledge and experiences. When we are curious, we open ourselves up to new possibilities and perspectives. This is where creativity begins.

Children are naturally curious, always asking "why" and "how" as they try to make sense of the world around them. Unfortunately, as we grow older, many of us lose this sense of wonder and inquiry, settling into routines and patterns that limit our creative thinking. But the good news is that curiosity can be reignited at any stage of life.

To foster creativity, it's essential to cultivate a mindset of curiosity. This means asking questions, seeking out new experiences, and being open to learning from a wide range of sources. The more curious we are, the more connections we can make between seemingly unrelated ideas, leading to greater creative insights.

Developing a Creative Mindset

Finally, developing a creative mindset is about more than just curiosity—it's about embracing the process of exploration and experimentation. A creative mindset is one that welcomes uncertainty and is willing to take risks. It involves letting go of the fear of failure and understanding that mistakes are an essential part of the creative journey.

Creativity flourishes when we are willing to step outside of our comfort zones and try new things. This might mean approaching problems from a different angle, experimenting with new methods, or challenging assumptions. It requires a willingness to be vulnerable and to trust in the process, even when the outcome is unclear.

By cultivating curiosity and embracing the uncertainty that comes with creativity, we open ourselves up to a world of possibilities. We learn to see challenges as opportunities and obstacles as invitations to think differently. In doing so, we unlock the full potential of our creativity and set the stage for innovation.

In summary, understanding the foundations of creativity is the first step in fostering it in our lives. Creativity is not a rare gift possessed by a few but a skill that everyone can develop. By embracing curiosity, debunking myths, and developing a creative mindset, we can tap into our creative potential and use it to enhance both our personal and professional lives. Creativity is not just about art—it's about approaching life with an open mind, a sense of wonder, and a willingness to explore new possibilities.

Building a Creative Environment

Creativity doesn't happen in a vacuum. It flourishes in environments that encourage exploration, experimentation, and free thinking. Whether it's your physical surroundings, the social atmosphere you operate in, or your mental state, the right environment can be the catalyst for creative breakthroughs. If we want to foster creativity in our lives, we must first take a close look at the spaces we inhabit—both external and internal—and consider how they influence our ability to think creatively.

Creating a Physical Space That Sparks Creativity

The physical space where you spend your time can have a significant impact on your creative output. A cluttered, noisy, or overly restrictive environment can stifle creativity, while a space that is open, organized, and stimulating can inspire fresh ideas and innovative thinking. This is why many creative professionals—writers, artists, designers—often speak of the importance of their workspaces. The right physical environment can help you get into a creative flow more easily.

One of the first steps in building a creative environment is de-cluttering. A cluttered space can lead to a cluttered mind, making it difficult to focus on generating new ideas. Tidying up your space, organizing your materials, and removing unnecessary distractions can clear the way for more creative thinking. However, it's important to strike a balance—some people thrive in spaces that are filled with visual inspiration, like artwork or creative tools. The key is to create a space that works for you personally.

In addition to keeping your workspace organized, consider the sensory elements of your environment. Lighting, for instance, can have a profound impact on creativity. Natural light has been shown to improve mood and cognitive function, while dim lighting can encourage more abstract thinking. Similarly, sound plays a role—some people work best in silence, while others find that ambient noise or music can stimulate creativity.

Personalizing your space is another way to cultivate creativity. Surround yourself with objects that inspire you—whether it's art, books, plants, or photos that spark positive emotions. These personal touches can help to create an environment that feels conducive to creative exploration and experimentation.

Fostering Creativity in a Collaborative Environment

While physical space is important, the social environment you're in can be just as influential. Whether you're working on a team or collaborating with others in your personal life, the atmosphere of openness and trust is crucial for creative growth. When people feel safe to express ideas, even ones that seem far-fetched or unconventional, creativity thrives.

To foster a collaborative environment that promotes creativity, it's important to encourage open communication and active listening. In settings where individuals feel valued and heard, they are more likely to share their ideas without fear of judgment. This openness often leads to the generation of more innovative ideas, as people build on one another's suggestions and perspectives.

A key aspect of a creative social environment is embracing diversity—of thought, experience, and perspective. When people from different backgrounds come together to solve a problem or brainstorm new ideas, the chances of arriving at a creative solution increase dramatically. Encourage diverse voices in your teams and social circles, as they bring different ways of thinking and seeing the world, which can lead to new, creative approaches.

Creating a culture that celebrates creativity also involves making room for failure. In environments where mistakes are seen as learning opportunities rather than setbacks, people are more willing to take risks and explore unconventional ideas. When people feel safe to fail, they are more likely to think outside the box and push creative boundaries.

Balancing Structure and Freedom

One of the paradoxes of creativity is that it requires both structure and freedom. Too much structure can stifle creative thinking, while too much freedom can lead to chaos and lack of focus. The key is to find the right balance that allows for both exploration and productivity.

Structure provides a framework for creativity. It gives us boundaries within which we can innovate. For example, setting specific goals or deadlines can help direct your creative energy and prevent you from becoming overwhelmed by too many possibilities. At the same time, it's important to allow for freedom within that structure—time and space to explore ideas without the pressure of immediate judgment or perfection.

One way to balance structure and freedom is through time management. Setting aside specific times for brainstorming or creative work can create a routine that supports consistent creative output. However, during these times, it's essential to allow yourself to explore without strict guidelines. This could mean allowing yourself to think freely for an hour without trying to come up with a perfect solution, or taking a break from a project to pursue a new idea that excites you.

In group settings, balancing structure and freedom might involve creating an agenda for a brainstorming session but allowing for flexibility in the direction the conversation takes. It could also mean establishing clear roles and responsibilities while encouraging team members to think creatively within those boundaries.

Reducing Distractions to Foster Focus

In today's hyper-connected world, distractions are one of the biggest obstacles to creativity. With constant notifications, emails, and social media vying for our attention, it's easy to lose focus and derail the creative process. To foster creativity, it's essential to reduce these distractions and create an environment where deep work can happen.

One strategy is to designate specific times when you turn off notifications and focus solely on creative tasks. This might mean setting your phone on "Do Not Disturb" mode, closing unnecessary browser tabs, or working in a quiet space where you won't be interrupted. Creating boundaries around your time allows you to enter a state of flow, where you can fully immerse yourself in the creative process.

Another helpful approach is to minimize multitasking. While it may seem efficient, multitasking often divides your attention and makes it harder to think creatively. Focusing on one task at a time allows you to engage more deeply with the problem at hand, leading to more original and well-thought-out ideas.

Conclusion: The Power of the Right Environment

Building a creative environment is about more than just changing your physical space—it's about creating the right conditions, both externally and internally, to encourage creative thinking. By designing a workspace that inspires you, fostering a culture of openness and collaboration, balancing structure with freedom, and reducing distractions, you can create an environment that allows creativity to thrive.

Ultimately, creativity is not something that happens in isolation. It is deeply influenced by the world around us. By taking control of our environment—whether that's our home office, our team dynamics, or our mental habits—we can shape the conditions that allow creativity to flourish. In doing so, we unlock our potential to innovate, problem-solve, and bring new ideas to life.

Cultivating a Growth Mindset for Creativity

At the core of fostering creativity lies the belief that you can become more creative through effort, learning, and practice. This is where the concept of a *growth mindset* comes into play. A term coined by psychologist Carol Dweck, a growth mindset is the belief that abilities and intelligence can be developed with time and dedication, as opposed to a *fixed mindset*, which assumes that these qualities are innate and unchangeable.

When it comes to creativity, adopting a growth mindset is essential. Many people believe that creativity is an inborn talent, something that only artists, musicians, or inventors possess. However, creativity is a skill that can be cultivated by anyone willing to put in the work. Shifting from a fixed mindset to a growth mindset opens the door to continual improvement, experimentation, and innovation.

Embracing Challenges as Opportunities for Growth

A fundamental aspect of a growth mindset is viewing challenges not as threats but as opportunities to learn and grow. Creativity often thrives in the face of obstacles, but only if we're willing to embrace those obstacles instead of avoiding them. The fear of failure can be a significant roadblock to creativity, especially for those who hold a fixed mindset. If you believe that your creative abilities are limited, you may be less likely to take risks or try new things, fearing that failure will confirm your limitations.

In contrast, individuals with a growth mindset see failure as part of the creative process. They understand that every misstep is an opportunity to learn something new, refine their approach, and ultimately grow. This mindset encourages experimentation—knowing that not every idea will be a winner, but each attempt will bring you closer to success.

For example, Thomas Edison is famous for his growth mindset approach to invention. When asked about his numerous failed attempts to create the lightbulb, he responded, "I have not failed. I've just found 10,000 ways that won't work." His persistence in the face of failure exemplifies the power of a growth mindset in fostering creativity. By embracing challenges and viewing them as stepping stones rather than roadblocks, you allow yourself the freedom to think outside the box and pursue unconventional solutions.

Shifting from a Fixed to a Growth Mindset

Shifting from a fixed to a growth mindset requires conscious effort, especially if you've spent years believing that creativity is something you either have or don't. The first step is recognizing and challenging limiting beliefs about your creative potential. You might think, "I'm just not a creative person," or "I can't come up with original ideas." These are classic fixed mindset statements that reinforce the belief that creativity is a fixed trait.

To cultivate a growth mindset, replace these limiting beliefs with empowering ones. Instead of saying, "I'm not creative," try saying, "I can develop my creativity with practice." Instead of thinking, "I'll never come up with a good idea," remind yourself, "The more I experiment and explore, the more creative ideas I'll generate." These simple shifts in language and self-talk can have a profound impact on how you approach creative challenges.

Another powerful way to reinforce a growth mindset is to celebrate the process of learning and improvement rather than focusing solely on the end result. In creative work, it's easy to get discouraged if an idea doesn't work out or if the final product isn't as polished as you'd hoped. However, by valuing the effort you put into the process, you begin to see each step as progress, even if it's not perfect.

Seeking Feedback and Embracing Constructive Criticism

A hallmark of a growth mindset is the willingness to seek feedback and use it as a tool for improvement. People with a fixed mindset often avoid feedback because they fear it will expose their perceived shortcomings. They may see criticism as a reflection of their limitations rather than as a valuable opportunity to learn and grow.

In contrast, those with a growth mindset actively seek feedback, knowing that constructive criticism can help them refine their ideas and improve their creative abilities. Embracing feedback doesn't mean accepting all criticism without question, but it does mean being open to different perspectives and considering how they can inform your creative process.

One way to embrace feedback is by approaching it with curiosity rather than defensiveness. Instead of viewing criticism as a personal attack, see it as an opportunity to learn something new about your work and how it can be improved. Ask questions, seek clarification, and use the feedback as a tool for growth. Remember, the goal of feedback is not to confirm your existing abilities, but to help you push the boundaries of your creativity.

In creative fields, feedback can often spark new ideas and perspectives that you hadn't considered before. It can challenge your assumptions, broaden your thinking, and lead to unexpected innovations. By seeking out and embracing feedback, you can continually refine your creative process and produce work that is more thoughtful, polished, and impactful.

The Role of Persistence and Patience in Creativity

One of the key traits of a growth mindset is persistence. Creative breakthroughs rarely happen overnight, and the path to innovation is often filled with setbacks, revisions, and moments of doubt. People with a fixed mindset may give up at the first sign of difficulty, believing that their creative abilities are limited. However, those with a growth mindset understand that creativity requires patience and perseverance.

The creative process can be frustrating at times, especially when progress feels slow or when you encounter roadblocks. But persistence is what separates successful creatives from those who give up too soon. By sticking with a project, continuing to iterate on your ideas, and pushing through challenges, you increase the likelihood of arriving at a solution that is truly innovative.

The creative journey is not a straight line—it's filled with twists, turns, and unexpected detours. It requires a willingness to keep going, even when the outcome is uncertain. The more you practice persistence in your creative endeavors, the more resilient and adaptable you become, which in turn fuels even greater creativity.

Conclusion: Cultivating Creativity Through a Growth Mindset

In conclusion, a growth mindset is essential for unlocking your creative potential. By embracing challenges, seeking feedback, and persisting through setbacks, you can develop your creativity over time. Creativity is not a fixed trait; it's a skill that can be nurtured through effort, practice, and a willingness to learn from both success and failure. By shifting from a fixed to a growth mindset, you open yourself up to new possibilities and allow your creativity to flourish in ways you never thought possible.

Creating an Environment that Nurtures Innovation

A key factor in fostering creativity is the environment in which you work and live. Whether physical or psychological, your environment plays a significant role in how easily you can access your creative potential. A cluttered, chaotic space may distract you from focusing on your ideas, while a judgmental or rigid atmosphere may stifle your willingness to take creative risks. Understanding how to create an environment that nurtures innovation can have a profound impact on your ability to think freely, experiment, and ultimately bring new ideas to life.

The Power of a Physical Environment

Your physical surroundings have a direct influence on your state of mind, and consequently, your ability to be creative. For many people, working in a cluttered or overly structured environment can impede creativity. A cluttered workspace might lead to a cluttered mind, making it harder to focus and generate new ideas. On the other hand, a well-organized, inspiring space can encourage a free flow of thoughts.

Consider the atmosphere of famous creative spaces throughout history. Artists like Pablo Picasso and writers like Virginia Woolf often spoke of the importance of their studios and work environments as part of their creative process. A serene, quiet space filled with inspiring objects can serve as a catalyst for innovation. The presence of plants, natural light, or aesthetically pleasing decor can stimulate creative thinking, while noise-canceling tools or background music may help you focus.

However, it's important to understand that creativity is personal, and what works for one person might not work for another. Some people thrive in environments filled with visual stimulation, while others need a minimalist approach. The key is to create a workspace that fosters your unique style of creativity. Whether it's adding a splash of color, incorporating elements from nature, or simply decluttering, curating your space with intentionality can significantly boost your creative output.

Designing for Flexibility and Exploration

A creative environment doesn't just refer to your physical workspace; it also encompasses how you structure your time and activities. Flexibility is essential for innovation because creativity doesn't always follow a linear process. Rigid schedules, repetitive routines, and overly structured time management can suffocate the creative process. Instead, building in time for exploration, experimentation, and play can unlock new possibilities.

Giving yourself the freedom to explore different ideas without judgment or time pressure is a critical component of innovation. Many breakthroughs happen when people allow themselves to take mental detours, entertain "wild" ideas, and follow seemingly unrelated threads of thought. For example, the concept of "structured procrastination" suggests that when you give yourself permission to explore ideas freely, even when it doesn't seem productive, you often stumble upon creative insights that lead to greater achievements.

Flexible environments foster curiosity, and curiosity is the bedrock of innovation. This might mean setting aside regular blocks of time for brainstorming, or creating spaces where you can experiment with ideas without the fear of failure. Whether it's a dedicated time for creative activities like writing, sketching, or problem-solving, building flexibility into your routine can enhance your capacity to innovate.

Encouraging a Culture of Openness and Collaboration

Creativity doesn't happen in isolation. While individual innovation is important, many of the world's greatest ideas emerged through collaboration. Surrounding yourself with people who support and challenge your thinking can be one of the most effective ways to nurture creativity. This is true whether you're in a workplace, a community, or even in your personal relationships.

Creating an environment of psychological safety—where people feel free to express unconventional ideas without judgment—is crucial for fostering innovation. In an environment where people are afraid to make mistakes or be ridiculed, creativity is often stifled. But when you surround yourself with individuals who encourage open dialogue and constructive feedback, you create a space where ideas can flourish.

For example, companies like Google and Pixar have built their success on fostering collaborative environments that prioritize creativity. These organizations encourage employees to engage in open-ended brainstorming sessions, participate in interdisciplinary teams, and give feedback without fear of criticism. By fostering a culture of openness and collaboration, they have created spaces where groundbreaking innovations happen regularly.

Whether you are working alone or within a group, it's important to create an environment where exploration is encouraged and failure is seen as part of the creative process. Surrounding yourself with people who inspire and challenge you to think in new ways can lead to unexpected insights and breakthroughs.

Reducing Mental Clutter and Distractions

In our hyperconnected world, distractions are one of the biggest threats to creativity. Social media notifications, constant emails, and the barrage of digital noise can make it difficult to focus on creative work. Studies show that multitasking can significantly reduce cognitive function and the ability to produce high-quality work, especially in tasks requiring deep concentration, such as creative problem-solving.

Reducing distractions and mental clutter is essential for fostering an environment that supports creativity. This might mean turning off notifications during creative work, setting boundaries for social media use, or creating "distraction-free" zones in your home or office. In some cases, it might also mean simplifying your commitments so that you have more mental bandwidth for innovation.

By eliminating distractions and streamlining your focus, you give your brain the space it needs to engage in deep, uninterrupted thinking—a state where creativity truly thrives. Many successful creatives, from authors to entrepreneurs, have daily routines that prioritize uninterrupted blocks of time for creative work. Whether it's early in the morning or late at night, identifying the times and places where you can work free of distraction is key to nurturing innovation.

Balancing Structure with Freedom

While creativity thrives in flexibility, it's also important to find the right balance between structure and freedom. Too much structure can stifle creativity, but too little structure can lead to chaos and a lack of focus. Successful creatives often find a rhythm that combines periods of unstructured exploration with moments of disciplined focus.

For example, you might dedicate certain times of the day to free-form brainstorming or spontaneous idea generation, while also scheduling structured periods for refining and executing those ideas. This balance allows you to enjoy the benefits of both worlds—giving your creativity space to roam freely, while also ensuring that your innovations can be brought to fruition.

The balance between structure and freedom is personal, and it may take some trial and error to discover what works best for you. By experimenting with different approaches, you'll eventually find the balance that allows your creativity to flow while maintaining the discipline needed to turn ideas into reality.

Conclusion: Designing for Creative Success

Your environment is a reflection of your mindset, and by intentionally shaping your surroundings—whether physical, mental, or social—you can create an ecosystem that nurtures creativity. From curating a space that inspires, to building a culture of openness and collaboration, every aspect of your environment plays a role in your ability to innovate. By reducing distractions, embracing flexibility, and finding the right balance between structure and freedom, you can design an environment that fosters creativity and allows you to realize your full creative potential.

Sustaining Long-Term Creativity and Innovation

Creativity isn't a one-time event; it's a continuous process that requires sustained effort, energy, and nurturing over time. Just like any other skill, your ability to be creative and innovative must be cultivated regularly to maintain its strength. The challenge for many people is not just in generating new ideas, but in sustaining the flow of creativity and turning those ideas into lasting, impactful innovations. To keep your creative momentum alive, it's essential to establish habits and strategies that enable long-term success.

Building a Routine for Creativity

One of the most effective ways to sustain creativity over time is to build it into your routine. While creativity might seem spontaneous or unpredictable, many highly creative people rely on consistent habits that allow them to generate new ideas regularly. Whether it's daily brainstorming sessions, journaling, or setting aside time for creative projects, having a structured routine ensures that you're continuously feeding your creative energy.

For example, novelist Haruki Murakami follows a strict daily routine where he wakes up early to write for several hours before engaging in other activities. This regularity helps him stay in the creative flow, even on days when inspiration doesn't come easily. Similarly, designer and entrepreneur Tim Ferriss advocates for regular "idea sprints," where you dedicate short, focused bursts of time to generate as many ideas as possible. These routines create the structure necessary to sustain creativity and ensure that it becomes a habit rather than a rare occurrence.

By embedding creativity into your daily or weekly schedule, you not only maintain your innovative mindset but also build the resilience to overcome creative blocks when they arise. Consistency, more than talent or inspiration, is often the key to producing truly innovative work.

Prioritizing Rest and Recovery

While consistency is important, it's equally essential to recognize the value of rest and recovery in sustaining long-term creativity. Creativity requires mental energy, and burnout is a real threat to those who push themselves too hard without taking time to recharge. Many people make the mistake of believing that working longer hours or forcing themselves to generate new ideas will lead to better results, but this often leads to diminishing returns.

The brain, like any muscle, needs time to rest in order to perform at its best. Research shows that taking regular breaks, getting enough sleep, and engaging in restorative activities can significantly improve creative thinking and problem-solving abilities. This is why many creatives and innovators, from artists to tech entrepreneurs, prioritize activities like meditation, exercise, and time spent in nature to refresh their minds.

By scheduling time for rest and mental recovery, you create the space needed for ideas to incubate. This downtime allows your subconscious mind to process information and make connections that may not be immediately apparent when you're actively working. It's often during moments of relaxation or when your mind is wandering that creative breakthroughs occur.

Embracing Failure as Part of the Process

Creativity and innovation inherently involve risk-taking, and with that comes the likelihood of failure. Whether it's an idea that doesn't pan out or a project that falls short of expectations, failure is an inevitable part of the creative journey. What distinguishes successful innovators from those who give up is their ability to embrace failure as a learning opportunity rather than a setback.

Some of the world's greatest innovators, from Thomas Edison to Steve Jobs, experienced significant failures before achieving success. Edison famously tested thousands of prototypes before inventing the lightbulb, and Jobs was once ousted from the very company he founded. Yet, both viewed failure as a stepping stone toward eventual success, using it to refine their ideas and improve their approaches.

To sustain long-term creativity, it's crucial to adopt a mindset that welcomes failure as part of the process. Instead of fearing mistakes, view them as valuable feedback that guides you toward better solutions. When you embrace failure, you build resilience and the ability to persist through challenges—traits that are essential for sustaining innovation over time.

Collaborating with Others for Fresh Perspectives

Creativity doesn't thrive in isolation. Often, the most innovative ideas come from collaboration and interaction with others. Surrounding yourself with a diverse group of thinkers, creatives, and problem-solvers can provide fresh perspectives that help you see your work in new ways. Whether through formal collaborations, brainstorming sessions, or simply engaging in conversations with people outside your field, interacting with others can spark new ideas and inspire creative growth.

Many companies, from tech startups to design firms, actively foster environments where collaboration is encouraged. This cross-pollination of ideas often leads to breakthrough innovations, as individuals with different experiences and skill sets bring unique insights to the table. For example, the partnership between Steve Jobs and designer Jony Ive at Apple resulted in some of the most iconic and innovative products in tech history, from the iPhone to the MacBook.

By seeking out collaboration and being open to input from others, you create opportunities to build on your ideas and push them further than you could on your own. Collaboration not only sustains creativity but also accelerates innovation by combining the strengths of multiple minds.

Staying Curious and Continuously Learning

At the heart of sustained creativity is a mindset of curiosity and lifelong learning. Innovation is not a destination but a continuous journey of exploration and discovery. The more you expose yourself to new ideas, knowledge, and experiences, the more you fuel your creative engine. This means staying curious, asking questions, and seeking out opportunities to learn from others and from the world around you.

Many creative individuals make it a habit to explore fields outside their own areas of expertise. For example, renowned chef Ferran Adrià, known for his avant-garde culinary creations, drew inspiration not only from food but also from art, science, and technology. By continuously learning and exposing yourself to new sources of inspiration, you expand the range of possibilities for innovation.

To maintain long-term creativity, cultivate the habit of learning something new every day. Whether it's reading a book, attending a workshop, or simply observing the world around you, these moments of learning keep your mind open and receptive to new ideas. Creativity thrives on diversity of thought, and by staying curious, you ensure that your innovative spirit remains vibrant over time.

Conclusion: The Long Road of Innovation

Sustaining creativity and innovation over the long term requires a combination of habits, mindset shifts, and intentional practices. By building creativity into your routine, prioritizing rest, embracing failure, collaborating with others, and staying curious, you can create a sustainable foundation for ongoing innovation. The road to lasting creativity is a marathon, not a sprint, and with the right strategies in place, you can continue to generate fresh ideas and bring them to life for years to come.

{ **10** }

Chapter 10: Networking and Building Relationships

The Importance of Networking for Personal and Professional Growth

Networking is often misunderstood as a superficial exchange of business cards or LinkedIn connections, but its true essence goes far deeper. At its core, networking is about building relationships that can enhance your life both personally and professionally. Whether you're seeking to grow in your career, expand your knowledge, or simply connect with like-minded individuals, the relationships you foster through networking can serve as the foundation for much of your success.

In the modern world, your network often acts as a bridge to new opportunities. It's no longer just about what you know; it's about who you know and how well you maintain those relationships. A well-connected person often has access to a wealth of knowledge, support, and opportunities that might not be available through formal channels. Job opportunities, partnerships, advice, and personal growth are just a few examples of how your network can open doors that otherwise might remain closed.

But beyond professional advancement, networking also plays a crucial role in personal development. The people you surround

{ 177 }

yourself with can inspire you, challenge you, and push you toward new heights. Relationships built on trust and mutual respect can offer not only career boosts but also emotional and intellectual support. This is why it's essential to look at networking as more than just a transactional activity but rather as an ongoing process of building relationship capital—an investment in people that pays dividends over time.

Take for instance the story of Sarah, a marketing professional who was feeling stuck in her job. She attended a conference, initially unsure of what she hoped to gain. During one of the networking breaks, she struck up a conversation with a speaker who shared insights about her own career journey. This casual connection eventually turned into a mentorship, helping Sarah gain the confidence and skills to transition into a higher role within her company. In another instance, Sarah connected with someone from a completely different industry who introduced her to a broader perspective on creative marketing strategies, which she later applied to her work. The value of networking became clear to Sarah when these seemingly unrelated connections began influencing her personal and professional growth in ways she hadn't anticipated.

The power of networking extends beyond the initial connection. It's about the long-term relationships you foster and how those relationships enrich your life. When you invest time in building and maintaining your network, you're not only creating opportunities for career progression but also broadening your horizons and developing a community that supports your growth.

A key benefit of networking is the access it provides to diverse perspectives and ideas. When you connect with individuals from different backgrounds, industries, and cultures, you're exposed to new ways of thinking. This diversity is a critical driver of personal growth because it challenges your assumptions and broadens your worldview. In a professional context, these varied perspectives can lead to innovation, helping you to approach problems from angles you might not have considered before. In a personal context, they encourage empathy and understanding, allowing you to form deeper, more meaningful connections.

Networking is not limited to extroverts or those in high-profile careers. Anyone can benefit from building and nurturing a network, regardless of their personality or profession. The key is to approach networking with an open mind and a genuine interest in others. It's not about what someone can do for you right away, but rather how you can support each other over time. When approached with authenticity, networking becomes less about the exchange of favors and more about the exchange of value.

In conclusion, the importance of networking cannot be overstated when it comes to both personal and professional growth. Whether you're looking to advance your career, expand your knowledge, or simply form meaningful connections, your network will play a crucial role in achieving those goals. The relationships you build today could open doors for you tomorrow, making networking one of the most valuable investments you can make in your future.

Cultivating Authentic Relationships

When it comes to networking, many people make the mistake of treating it as a numbers game—believing that the more connections they have, the better off they'll be. However, the true strength of networking lies not in the quantity of relationships but in their quality. Cultivating authentic relationships is the foundation of meaningful networking. It's about building trust, respect, and genuine connections with others, rather than merely collecting contacts.

An authentic relationship in networking is one that is built on mutual respect and shared interests. It's not about approaching someone with the intent of getting something from them, but rather about fostering a connection that benefits both parties over time. People can sense when a relationship is transactional, and those are the types of connections that quickly fizzle out. On the other hand, when you approach networking with sincerity and a genuine desire to get to know someone, the relationship has a far better chance of lasting and becoming mutually rewarding.

One key to cultivating authenticity is to be present and engaged when interacting with others. When you meet someone new, listen actively to what they have to say rather than focusing on what you'll say next. Show genuine interest in their story, ask thoughtful questions, and be attentive to their responses. People are drawn to those who make them feel heard and understood. By being fully engaged in the conversation, you demonstrate that you value the person beyond what they can offer you professionally.

Take for example, the case of David, a young entrepreneur who attended various industry events with the sole intention of handing out as many business cards as possible. He would introduce himself, share a quick elevator pitch, and move on to the next person, hoping that sheer volume would translate into opportunities. However, David quickly realized that the connections he was making were shallow, and most of the people he met barely remembered him after the event.

Frustrated, David changed his approach. He decided to focus on cultivating fewer, but more meaningful, relationships. At the next event he attended, he spent more time engaging in deeper conversations with a handful of individuals, learning about their challenges, goals, and experiences. One of those individuals ended up becoming a business mentor to David, offering invaluable advice and guidance as he navigated the early stages of his career. That relationship would have never materialized if David had stuck to his original approach of superficial networking.

Another essential aspect of authentic networking is being genuine about your own story and intentions. Too often, people feel the need to project an image of success or competence that doesn't align with their current reality. They might exaggerate their accomplishments or downplay their struggles in an attempt to impress others. However, authenticity comes from being honest about who you are and where you are on your journey. People appreciate vulnerability, and it often opens the door for deeper connections. When you're transparent about your challenges, you create space for others to share their own, which fosters a sense of trust and camaraderie.

For instance, being upfront about the areas where you're still learning or growing can lead to mentorship opportunities, as others may see an opportunity to share their expertise. At the same time, when you're authentic, you're more likely to attract people who align with your values, leading to relationships that feel more natural and supportive.

Additionally, giving is a critical component of cultivating authentic relationships. Networking isn't just about what you can gain, but also about how you can contribute to others. Being generous with your time, knowledge, and resources creates a foundation of reciprocity. When you give without expecting anything in return, you build goodwill and trust, both of which are essential for long-term relationships. This could be as simple as introducing two people who could benefit from knowing each other or offering a helpful piece of advice when someone is facing a challenge.

Ultimately, the goal of authentic networking is to create relationships that are mutually beneficial and sustainable over time. As you build your network, focus on being genuine, engaged, and generous. Authentic connections don't just lead to opportunities—they enrich your personal and professional life in ways that transactional relationships never can. These are the connections that will stand the test of time, providing support, collaboration, and friendship throughout your journey.

In conclusion, cultivating authentic relationships in networking is about approaching people with sincerity and a genuine desire to connect. When you focus on building trust, being yourself, and giving as much as you receive, you lay the foundation for meaningful, lasting relationships. Authentic networking goes beyond professional gain; it becomes a source of personal growth and fulfillment, creating a network that truly supports and elevates you.

The Power of Mutual Support and Collaboration

One of the most profound benefits of networking is the potential for mutual support and collaboration. When done authentically, networking allows individuals to connect in ways that go beyond mere professional gain, creating relationships that foster growth, mentorship, and shared success. In a world where competition often takes center stage, the power of collaboration is frequently underestimated. Yet, when people come together, combining their strengths and resources, they can achieve far more than they could individually.

At the heart of any strong network is the principle of mutual support. This is the understanding that relationships are not one-sided but rather built on a foundation of give-and-take. When you help others succeed, you're not only contributing to their growth but also strengthening your own network and reputation.

People remember those who support them, and this creates a cycle of generosity and reciprocity that benefits everyone involved.

For instance, consider the case of Emily, a graphic designer who had spent years freelancing and building her portfolio. She connected with James, a web developer, through a local networking event. Initially, their conversations revolved around their respective work, but over time, they realized there was an opportunity for collaboration. Emily's design skills complemented James's web development expertise, and they decided to partner on a few projects. Their collaboration not only enhanced the quality of their work but also allowed them to offer more comprehensive services to clients, leading to more business for both. What started as a simple networking connection turned into a mutually beneficial partnership that elevated both of their careers.

Mutual support also extends to mentorship and guidance. As you grow in your career, you'll inevitably encounter situations where you could benefit from the advice and experience of others. Networking provides access to a wealth of knowledge from people who have been where you are or who have navigated similar challenges. Similarly, as you gain experience, you have the opportunity to offer guidance to those just starting out, creating a cycle of learning and support.

It's important to remember that mutual support doesn't always have to come in the form of direct collaboration or mentorship. Sometimes, it's as simple as offering a word of encouragement, sharing a resource, or making an introduction to someone who can help. These small acts of support build trust and goodwill, strengthening the bonds within your network. In fact, some of the most valuable connections are those built on mutual respect and support, without an immediate transactional benefit.

Over time, these relationships often yield unexpected opportunities and growth.

Another key aspect of mutual support is the way it encourages the sharing of ideas. Collaboration fosters innovation because it brings together diverse perspectives and skill sets. When individuals from different backgrounds, industries, or areas of expertise come together, they can approach problems from multiple angles, leading to creative solutions that might not have been possible in isolation. This is why networking across industries is so powerful—it allows you to tap into a broader range of ideas and insights, which can inspire new approaches to your own work.

For example, entrepreneurs often form mastermind groups, where members regularly meet to discuss their challenges, share advice, and brainstorm solutions. These groups are built on mutual support, with each person contributing their expertise and learning from the others. Through these collaborative discussions, participants gain new insights, solve problems more effectively, and push each other toward greater success. The collective wisdom of the group often far exceeds what any one individual could achieve on their own.

Moreover, mutual support and collaboration can extend beyond professional success. Many of the strongest networking relationships are those that also offer personal support. Navigating the ups and downs of a career can be challenging, and having a network of people who understand your journey can provide a valuable source of encouragement and reassurance. These connections often lead to long-lasting friendships that provide not only career benefits but also emotional and social support.

One of the most effective ways to foster mutual support in your network is to adopt a mindset of abundance rather than scarcity. In a scarcity mindset, you may view others as competitors and fear that helping someone else could diminish your own chances of success. But in an abundance mindset, you recognize that there's enough opportunity for everyone, and by supporting others, you contribute to a larger community of success. This mindset shift allows you to approach networking with a spirit of generosity, which in turn attracts people who share similar values.

In conclusion, mutual support and collaboration are powerful forces within any network. By focusing on building relationships where both parties benefit, you create an environment of trust, learning, and shared success. Whether through collaboration on projects, offering mentorship, or simply providing encouragement, the support you give and receive within your network will elevate not only your career but also your personal growth. Networking is not a solo endeavor; it's a community-driven process, and when we come together to support one another, we all rise higher.

Developing Deep and Meaningful Connections

While it's easy to think of networking as a numbers game—attending events, handing out business cards, and collecting LinkedIn connections—true networking goes far deeper than surface-level interactions. At its core, networking is about developing meaningful relationships that stand the test of time, built on trust, authenticity, and mutual respect. Deep connections, as opposed to casual acquaintances, have the power to influence both your personal and professional life in profound ways.

To cultivate these kinds of relationships, you must shift your mindset from transactional networking to relational networking. Transactional networking focuses on what you can get from the other person, while relational networking is about creating value for both parties. It's about genuinely caring about the other person's success, taking the time to listen to their goals and challenges, and being willing to help without expecting immediate returns.

Consider this: how many times have you attended a networking event where the conversation felt forced, with each person waiting for an opportunity to talk about themselves? These superficial interactions rarely lead to anything meaningful because they lack depth and connection. In contrast, meaningful relationships come from engaging conversations where both parties are fully present, listening, and interested in each other's perspectives. When you take the time to truly understand someone, you're laying the foundation for a relationship that can grow into something significant over time.

One way to build deeper connections is through active listening. Active listening goes beyond hearing someone's words; it involves fully engaging with what they are saying, asking thoughtful questions, and showing genuine curiosity about their experiences. People can tell when you are truly interested in them versus when you're simply waiting for your turn to speak. By demonstrating that you value what the other person has to say, you foster trust and respect—key ingredients for any meaningful relationship.

For example, imagine meeting a potential business partner at a conference. Instead of jumping straight into discussing your own work, take the time to ask about their business, their challenges, and what excites them about their industry. Through this conversation, you might discover shared interests or goals, and by showing genuine curiosity, you'll create a much stronger connection than if you had simply pitched your own ideas from the start. People are far more likely to remember and value a conversation where they felt heard and understood.

Another important aspect of building deep connections is authenticity. Authenticity means being true to yourself in your interactions with others. In a world where people often feel pressure to present a polished version of themselves, authenticity can be a breath of fresh air. When you show up as your true self—open, honest, and vulnerable—you invite others to do the same. This creates an environment where real relationships can form, rather than superficial connections based on what you think the other person wants to see.

Authenticity also means being transparent about your intentions and boundaries. If you're looking to collaborate with someone, be upfront about what you're hoping to achieve and how you think you can work together. Conversely, if you're not in a position to help someone at the moment, it's okay to say so—being honest will build trust in the long run. People appreciate transparency because it allows them to engage with you on a deeper level, knowing exactly where you stand.

Additionally, investing time and effort into maintaining relationships is crucial for creating long-lasting connections. It's not enough to make a great first impression and then move on. Building meaningful relationships requires consistent communication, follow-up, and support. This doesn't mean you need to be in constant contact, but rather that you make an effort to check in periodically, offer help when you can, and stay updated on the other person's life and work. Sending a thoughtful message, sharing a useful resource, or even just congratulating them on a recent achievement can go a long way in keeping the connection alive.

A key factor in maintaining deep relationships is the concept of reciprocity—being willing to give as much as you receive. Networking isn't just about asking for favors when you need something; it's about being available to help others, even when there's no immediate benefit to you. By offering support, advice, or connections to those in your network, you build goodwill and strengthen the relationship. When people see that you're genuinely invested in their success, they'll be more likely to offer the same in return.

Lastly, don't underestimate the power of shared experiences in deepening relationships. Attending events, working on projects together, or even spending time socially outside of professional settings can create bonds that go beyond the workplace. Shared experiences create memories and a sense of camaraderie that can make the relationship feel more personal and meaningful. Whether it's collaborating on a challenging project or simply grabbing coffee and discussing life, these moments help build the foundation of trust and friendship.

In conclusion, developing deep and meaningful connections is the key to truly elevating your network. By focusing on building authentic relationships based on trust, active listening, and mutual respect, you'll create a strong network that supports both your professional and personal growth. Networking is not about collecting contacts; it's about cultivating relationships that enrich your life and lead to long-term success. When you prioritize depth over breadth, you'll find that the relationships you develop are far more valuable and fulfilling.

The Importance of Follow-Through in Networking

Building a network is not just about making initial connections; it's about what happens after that first meeting. Many people think that a handshake, a business card exchange, or a quick LinkedIn connection is enough. But the real value of networking comes from follow-through—the actions you take after meeting someone to nurture and grow the relationship. Consistent, thoughtful follow-through is what turns fleeting interactions into lasting, meaningful relationships.

One of the biggest mistakes people make in networking is failing to follow up after an initial interaction. Think about it: you attend a conference, meet some interesting people, have engaging conversations, and perhaps even exchange contact information. Then, life gets busy, and before you know it, months have passed without any follow-up. That initial connection, no matter how promising, fades away into a missed opportunity. This is why follow-through is essential. It keeps the conversation going, helps build rapport, and shows the other person that you are serious about maintaining the relationship.

The first step to effective follow-through is timing. Ideally, you should follow up within a few days of meeting someone. A brief message thanking them for their time and referencing a specific point from your conversation shows that you value the interaction. For example, you might write, "I really enjoyed our conversation about the trends in sustainable business at last week's conference. I'd love to keep in touch and explore ways we might collaborate in the future." This kind of message is personal, polite, and keeps the door open for further communication.

Another key to successful follow-through is consistency. Building a relationship takes time, and it's important to stay in touch periodically. This doesn't mean you need to constantly reach out, but rather that you maintain a presence in their life. You might check in every few months, send a message on a professional milestone, or share an article or resource you think they would find valuable. Small gestures of thoughtfulness can keep you on their radar and show that you're genuinely interested in their success.

Additionally, follow-through isn't just about staying in touch—it's about delivering on any promises or commitments you made during your initial interaction. If you offered to introduce them to someone in your network, make sure you do it. If you discussed collaborating on a project, follow up with concrete steps to move forward. Nothing undermines a relationship faster than making promises you don't keep. On the other hand, following through on your commitments builds trust and credibility, key components of any strong relationship.

For example, imagine you meet someone at a networking event and offer to connect them with a colleague who works in their industry. After the event, you send an introductory email linking them with your colleague. Not only does this fulfill your promise, but it also strengthens your relationship with both parties. Following through on commitments demonstrates reliability, which is a trait people value highly in their professional networks.

Beyond promises, following through also means being proactive in finding ways to add value to the relationship. Instead of waiting for the other person to reach out, take the initiative. If you come across a job opening that might interest them, share it. If you see that their company made a big announcement, send a congratulatory note. These small but meaningful actions show that you're invested in their success and are willing to put in the effort to maintain the relationship. People are much more likely to think of you positively when you consistently show that you care.

In networking, it's also important to recognize that follow-through is a two-way street. While it's crucial to be proactive and reliable, it's also necessary to respect the other person's time and boundaries. Not every follow-up needs to be a request for something. In fact, some of the most effective networking follow-ups are simply about staying in touch and maintaining a connection. Networking is not just about what you can get from someone but also about what you can give—and sometimes, the best gift is simply being a consistent, supportive presence.

Furthermore, technology has made follow-through easier than ever. With tools like LinkedIn, email reminders, and calendar apps, it's possible to stay organized and intentional in your follow-up efforts. You can set reminders to check in with people, track your conversations, and even organize your contacts based on the nature of your relationship. Using these tools helps ensure that you don't let important connections slip through the cracks.

One often-overlooked aspect of follow-through is expressing gratitude. A simple thank-you can go a long way in strengthening a professional relationship. If someone takes time out of their day to meet with you, offer advice, or connect you with someone in their network, be sure to show your appreciation. A heartfelt thank-you note or message shows that you value their time and effort, which will make them more likely to want to continue the relationship.

In conclusion, follow-through is the glue that holds networking together. It's the difference between a one-time encounter and a lasting relationship. By being timely, consistent, reliable, and proactive in your follow-up efforts, you can turn casual meetings into deep, meaningful connections. And as you nurture these relationships over time, you'll find that they become an invaluable part of both your personal and professional growth. Effective follow-through is not just about getting ahead in your career; it's about building a network of trust, support, and mutual respect that can elevate every aspect of your life.

Part 3: Sustaining Growth and Balance

Chapter 11: Mastering Emotional Intelligence

Understanding Emotional Intelligence (EI)

Emotional intelligence (EI) has become a key factor in defining success in both personal and professional spheres. Unlike traditional measures of intelligence, which focus on cognitive abilities like logic, reasoning, and problem-solving (often referred to as IQ), emotional intelligence refers to our ability to understand, manage, and influence emotions—both our own and those of others.

At its core, emotional intelligence is about how well you navigate the emotional landscape of everyday life. It's the difference between reacting impulsively to a stressful situation and responding thoughtfully. It's what allows you to empathize with a colleague who's going through a rough time, resolve conflicts in a way that strengthens relationships, and motivate yourself and others when the going gets tough.

The Five Components of Emotional Intelligence

To grasp the full scope of EI, we can break it down into five key components, as defined by psychologist Daniel Goleman: self-awareness, self-regulation, motivation, empathy, and social skills.

Each of these plays a distinct role in how we perceive, process, and act on emotional information.

1. **Self-Awareness**: This is the ability to recognize and understand your own emotions, including what triggers them and how they influence your thoughts and actions. Self-awareness is the foundation of emotional intelligence because it allows you to understand how your emotions impact your behavior and decision-making. For instance, knowing that you tend to get anxious before big meetings can help you prepare mentally and emotionally, so you're not caught off guard.

2. **Self-Regulation**: While self-awareness helps you understand your emotions, self-regulation allows you to control and manage them. This doesn't mean suppressing your feelings, but rather channeling them in a productive way. When you can regulate your emotions, you can stay calm under pressure, resist the urge to react impulsively, and remain flexible in challenging situations.

3. **Motivation**: Emotionally intelligent people are often highly motivated—not just by external rewards, but by an inner drive to achieve goals. This intrinsic motivation helps them remain resilient in the face of obstacles and setbacks. They are also more likely to set long-term goals and pursue them with passion, even when the road is difficult.

4. **Empathy**: Empathy is the ability to understand and share the feelings of others. It goes beyond just being compassionate; it involves recognizing how others feel and why they feel that way. In the workplace, empathy helps leaders build trust with their teams, fosters collaboration, and enables better conflict resolution.

5. **Social Skills**: The final piece of the emotional intelligence puzzle involves your ability to interact effectively with others. Social skills encompass a wide range of abilities, including communication, conflict management, and building rapport. Whether you're leading a team or working alongside others, strong social skills are crucial for creating positive and productive relationships.

Why Emotional Intelligence Matters

In today's fast-paced, highly competitive world, emotional intelligence is more important than ever. While technical skills and knowledge are crucial, the ability to manage your emotions and understand those of others can be a game-changer. People with high emotional intelligence are better equipped to handle stress, navigate change, and maintain strong relationships—both at work and in their personal lives.

For example, consider a leader who is technically brilliant but lacks emotional intelligence. They may make excellent decisions based on data and logic, but if they can't manage their emotions or connect with their team on a human level, they are unlikely to inspire loyalty or motivate others to perform at their best. On the other hand, a leader with high emotional intelligence can build trust, foster a positive work environment, and lead their team through challenges with empathy and resilience.

Emotional intelligence is also closely tied to personal well-being. Studies have shown that individuals with high EI tend to have lower levels of stress and anxiety, better mental health, and stronger, more fulfilling relationships. This is because they are more in tune with their emotions and better equipped to handle the ups and downs of life.

Developing Emotional Intelligence

The good news is that emotional intelligence isn't a fixed trait—it can be developed and strengthened over time. By increasing your awareness of your emotions, practicing self-regulation, and improving your ability to empathize with others, you can enhance your emotional intelligence and reap the benefits in both your personal and professional life.

As you move through this chapter, you'll begin to see how each component of EI can be applied to everyday situations. Whether you're striving for career success, improving your relationships, or simply aiming to become more self-aware, understanding and developing emotional intelligence is a powerful tool for personal growth. It's not just about being "smart" emotionally—it's about using that intelligence to lead a more balanced, effective, and fulfilling life.

Cultivating Self-Awareness

Self-awareness is the cornerstone of emotional intelligence. Without understanding your own emotions, it becomes nearly impossible to regulate them, let alone empathize with others or develop stronger social skills. But what does self-awareness actually look like in practice, and how can you cultivate it in your everyday life?

Self-awareness begins with the simple act of paying attention—to your thoughts, feelings, and behaviors. It's about recognizing how your emotions influence your actions and understanding the patterns that shape your life. By becoming more aware of these patterns, you can begin to make conscious choices that align with your values, goals, and overall well-being.

The Power of Emotional Insight

At its core, self-awareness is about emotional insight. This involves more than just knowing when you're happy, sad, or angry. It's about understanding the underlying causes of your emotions and how they affect your behavior. For example, you might feel frustrated during a meeting at work. Instead of brushing off that frustration, self-awareness invites you to ask deeper questions: *Why am I frustrated? Is it because I feel unheard? Or maybe I'm stressed about an upcoming deadline?*

This type of introspection allows you to pinpoint the root cause of your emotions, which in turn helps you manage them more effectively. Instead of reacting impulsively—perhaps by snapping at a colleague or withdrawing from the conversation—you can respond in a way that is thoughtful and aligned with your desired outcome.

Self-awareness also means recognizing your emotional triggers. We all have them—those specific situations, people, or even memories that provoke strong emotional reactions. Maybe you get defensive when you receive constructive feedback, or perhaps you feel anxious in large social gatherings. Whatever your triggers are, self-awareness allows you to acknowledge them without judgment. By doing so, you can develop strategies to manage your emotional responses, rather than letting them control you.

Practical Ways to Build Self-Awareness

Developing self-awareness doesn't happen overnight, but there are practical steps you can take to start cultivating this skill. Here are a few strategies to help you become more in tune with your emotions and behaviors:

1. **Mindfulness Meditation**: Mindfulness is a powerful tool for building self-awareness. It involves paying attention to the present moment without judgment. By practicing mindfulness meditation, you can observe your thoughts and emotions as they arise, allowing you to become more aware of your inner landscape. This practice not only helps you rec-

ognize your emotional states but also gives you the space to choose how to respond to them.

2. **Journaling**: Writing down your thoughts and feelings is another effective way to enhance self-awareness. Journaling allows you to reflect on your emotions, identify patterns, and gain insight into the causes of your reactions. By regularly recording your experiences, you can track your emotional journey over time, which can lead to deeper understanding and growth.

3. **Self-Reflection**: Set aside time each day or week for self-reflection. Ask yourself questions like: *How did I feel today? What events triggered certain emotions? How did I respond, and was it effective?* Reflecting on your day-to-day experiences helps you become more conscious of how your emotions shape your actions, and it allows you to make adjustments when necessary.

4. **Seek Feedback**: Sometimes, it's hard to see ourselves clearly. This is where feedback from others can be invaluable. Ask trusted friends, family members, or colleagues for their observations about your emotional responses and behaviors. How do they perceive your reactions in stressful situations? Are there areas where you could improve? Constructive feedback can help you uncover blind spots and gain a more complete picture of yourself.

The Benefits of Self-Awareness

Why is self-awareness so important? Because it's the foundation of emotional regulation, empathy, and effective communication. When you understand your emotions and how they influence your behavior, you're better equipped to manage those emotions in a healthy way. Instead of being controlled by your feelings, you can choose how to respond to them.

For example, if you know that you tend to get anxious before big presentations, self-awareness can help you prepare. Maybe you'll recognize the physical signs of anxiety—your heart racing, your palms sweating—and instead of letting those sensations overwhelm you, you can take steps to calm yourself. You might practice deep breathing, visualize a successful presentation, or remind yourself of past achievements. Self-awareness gives you the tools to respond to your emotions in a way that serves you, rather than letting them dictate your actions.

Self-awareness also strengthens your relationships. When you're aware of your emotional triggers and patterns, you're less likely to project your feelings onto others. You'll be able to communicate more openly and honestly about your needs and boundaries, which fosters trust and understanding in your personal and professional interactions.

Self-Awareness as a Lifelong Practice

Cultivating self-awareness is an ongoing process. As you grow and evolve, so too will your emotions and behaviors. The key is to remain curious and open to learning about yourself. There will be times when you slip up, when you react impulsively or let your emotions get the best of you. But each of these moments is an opportunity to learn, reflect, and grow.

By committing to the practice of self-awareness, you can become more attuned to your emotions, more intentional in your actions, and more aligned with your goals. Ultimately, self-awareness empowers you to live a more authentic, balanced, and fulfilling life.

Managing Your Emotions Effectively

Once you've developed self-awareness, the next step in mastering emotional intelligence is learning how to manage your emotions effectively. Emotional regulation isn't about suppressing or ignoring your feelings; it's about recognizing them, accepting them, and then responding to them in a way that aligns with your values and goals. When you can manage your emotions, you maintain control over your actions and reactions, even in the face of stress, frustration, or conflict.

Why Emotional Management Matters

Emotions are powerful forces that influence nearly every aspect of our lives. They affect how we perceive situations, how we interact with others, and how we make decisions. When you're able to manage your emotions, you're better equipped to handle challenges, maintain healthy relationships, and make thoughtful decisions—both personally and professionally.

On the flip side, when emotions go unmanaged, they can lead to impulsive reactions, misunderstandings, and regret. You might find yourself saying or doing things in the heat of the moment that you later wish you hadn't. For example, feeling angry during a disagreement at work might cause you to speak harshly to a colleague, damaging your relationship and creating unnecessary tension. Learning how to manage your emotions prevents these knee-jerk reactions and allows you to respond in a calm, constructive manner.

Recognizing and Naming Emotions

The first step to managing emotions is recognizing and naming them. It sounds simple, but many people struggle to accurately identify what they're feeling in the moment. Sometimes, emotions are layered—what appears as anger might actually be masking fear or frustration. Other times, the intensity of an emotion might make it difficult to pinpoint the exact feeling.

By taking a moment to pause and reflect on what you're experiencing, you give yourself the space to recognize the emotion. Ask yourself, *What am I feeling right now?* Be as specific as possible. Are you anxious, disappointed, embarrassed, or excited? The more accurately you can identify your emotions, the easier it becomes to manage them.

Naming your emotions is a powerful practice. Research has shown that simply labeling what you're feeling can help reduce the intensity of the emotion. When you acknowledge your feelings, you gain a sense of control over them, rather than allowing them to control you.

Techniques for Managing Emotions

Once you've identified what you're feeling, the next step is to manage those emotions. Here are a few practical techniques you can use to regulate your emotions in a healthy, productive way:

1. **Pause Before Reacting**: One of the most effective ways to manage emotions is to create space between the stimulus and your response. This means pausing before you react. Whether you're feeling angry, anxious, or overwhelmed, take a deep breath and give yourself a moment to reflect before responding. This brief pause allows you to gather your thoughts, consider your options, and choose a more measured response.

2. **Practice Deep Breathing**: When emotions run high, especially in moments of stress or frustration, your body's physiological response can exacerbate your feelings. Deep breathing is a simple yet powerful technique to calm your nervous system and regain control over your emotions. Take slow, deep breaths, inhaling through your nose and exhaling through your mouth. Focus on your breath, allowing

it to slow your heart rate and bring a sense of calm to your body and mind.

3. **Reframe the Situation**: Another effective strategy for managing emotions is cognitive reframing. This involves changing the way you interpret a situation to alter your emotional response. For example, if you receive critical feedback at work, your initial reaction might be to feel defensive or upset. But by reframing the situation, you can view the feedback as an opportunity for growth and improvement rather than a personal attack. Reframing allows you to shift your perspective and choose a more constructive emotional response.

4. **Channel Your Emotions into Action**: Emotions are a source of energy, and one of the best ways to manage them is to channel that energy into positive action. If you're feeling frustrated or stressed, engage in an activity that helps you release that emotion in a healthy way. This might include going for a walk, exercising, or working on a creative project. By directing your emotional energy into something productive, you not only manage the emotion but also create a sense of accomplishment and forward movement.

5. **Use Self-Compassion**: Managing emotions isn't about being perfect or never feeling upset. It's about recognizing when emotions arise and treating yourself with kindness as you navigate those feelings. Practicing self-compassion involves acknowledging that it's okay to feel whatever you're feeling, without judgment. When you treat yourself with patience and understanding, you're better equipped to manage difficult emotions and move forward in a positive direction.

Managing Emotions in High-Stress Situations

High-stress situations can test your emotional regulation skills. Whether it's a conflict at work, a personal setback, or a rapidly changing environment, these moments often evoke intense emotional responses. In these situations, it's crucial to rely on the emotional management techniques you've cultivated.

In the heat of the moment, remember to pause and assess the situation before reacting. Take deep breaths, and remind yourself that your emotional response is within your control. By doing so, you can maintain composure and respond in a way that aligns with your long-term goals.

For instance, if you're in the midst of a heated argument, rather than letting your emotions take over and saying something you might regret, you can choose to step away, cool down, and revisit the conversation when both parties are calmer. This not only prevents unnecessary escalation but also strengthens your ability to resolve conflicts constructively.

The Long-Term Benefits of Emotional Regulation

Learning to manage your emotions isn't just about handling day-to-day challenges. It has long-term benefits for your overall well-being. People who are skilled at emotional regulation tend to experience lower levels of stress, better mental health, and more fulfilling relationships. They're also more resilient, able to navigate adversity with grace and confidence.

Emotionally intelligent individuals are not immune to challenges, but they are equipped with the tools to handle them effectively. They can maintain a sense of balance and perspective, even in the face of difficulty, which allows them to stay focused on their goals and values.

Ultimately, managing your emotions is an ongoing practice. As with any skill, it requires time, patience, and dedication. But by consistently applying these techniques, you'll find that your emotional responses become more balanced, thoughtful, and aligned with the person you want to be. And in doing so, you'll elevate not only your emotional intelligence but also your personal and professional success.

Cultivating Empathy in Your Emotional Intelligence

Empathy is one of the foundational elements of emotional intelligence and a key factor in both personal and professional success. At its core, empathy is the ability to understand and share the feelings of others. It goes beyond simply recognizing what someone else is experiencing; it involves actively placing yourself in their shoes and responding with compassion and understanding.

In today's fast-paced world, where individual achievement is often prioritized, empathy can sometimes take a back seat. However, developing empathy enriches relationships, enhances communication, and fosters trust—making it an essential skill for anyone looking to elevate their emotional intelligence.

The Power of Empathy

Empathy allows you to connect with others on a deeper level. It helps you recognize when someone is feeling overwhelmed, stressed, or hurt, and it guides you to respond in a way that acknowledges their emotional experience. In both personal and professional settings, empathy leads to stronger, more meaningful connections, as people feel seen and understood.

When you respond to others with empathy, you create an environment of psychological safety. This is especially important in the workplace, where people may hesitate to share their true feelings or opinions. A leader or colleague who shows empathy encourages openness, collaboration, and creativity, as team members feel comfortable expressing their thoughts and concerns.

Moreover, empathy plays a crucial role in conflict resolution. In moments of disagreement, it's easy to become defensive or focused solely on your perspective. However, approaching conflict with empathy allows you to step back and consider the other person's viewpoint. By understanding their emotions and motivations, you're better equipped to find common ground and reach a resolution that benefits both parties.

The Three Types of Empathy

While empathy may seem like a singular concept, it actually manifests in different forms. Understanding these different types of empathy can help you develop a more well-rounded approach to connecting with others:

1. **Cognitive Empathy**: This is the ability to understand someone else's perspective or thought process. It involves thinking about how the other person might feel in a particular situation, without necessarily sharing their emotions. Cognitive empathy is often useful in professional settings, where it's important to understand the viewpoints and motivations of others without becoming emotionally overwhelmed.

2. **Emotional Empathy**: Also known as affective empathy, this type involves actually feeling what another person is feeling. If a friend is experiencing grief, for example, emotional empathy allows you to share in that sorrow, creating a deep emotional connection. While this type of empathy can be incredibly powerful, it also requires emotional regulation to prevent becoming overwhelmed by others' emotions.

3. **Compassionate Empathy**: This is the combination of cognitive and emotional empathy, paired with a desire to help. Compassionate empathy drives you to not only understand

and feel what another person is experiencing but also take action to support them. It's the type of empathy that compels you to offer a helping hand when someone is struggling, or to provide a listening ear when someone needs to talk.

How to Cultivate Empathy

Empathy is not something you either have or don't have—it's a skill that can be developed and strengthened over time. Here are a few strategies for cultivating empathy in your daily life:

1. **Active Listening**: One of the most important aspects of empathy is listening to understand, rather than listening to respond. In conversations, practice giving the other person your full attention without interrupting or jumping to conclusions. By truly listening to what they're saying, you'll gain a better understanding of their emotions and perspective.

Active listening also involves paying attention to nonverbal cues, such as body language and tone of voice. These signals can provide important insights into how someone is feeling, even if they're not explicitly stating it.

1. **Ask Questions**: To deepen your understanding of another person's feelings, don't be afraid to ask open-ended questions. These types of questions encourage the other person to share more about their experience, and they demonstrate that you're genuinely interested in their perspective.

For example, instead of asking, "Are you okay?" you might ask, "Can you tell me more about what you're going through?" This invites a more thoughtful response and helps you gain a clearer picture of their emotional state.

1. **Practice Perspective-Taking**: Empathy often requires you to step outside of your own worldview and consider someone else's point of view. This can be challenging, especially when their experiences or beliefs differ significantly from your own. However, by making a conscious effort to imagine what the other person might be feeling or thinking, you can build greater empathy.

A helpful exercise is to ask yourself, *If I were in their shoes, how would I feel?* This simple shift in perspective can lead to greater understanding and more compassionate responses.

1. **Share Your Own Vulnerabilities**: Empathy is a two-way street. When you're open about your own feelings and vulnerabilities, you invite others to do the same. Sharing your experiences—whether it's a personal challenge or a moment of uncertainty—fosters mutual understanding and trust.

Of course, sharing doesn't mean overwhelming others with your problems, but rather finding moments of connection where you can relate to what someone else is going through. For instance, if a colleague is feeling stressed about a tight deadline, you might share a time when you faced a similar situation and how you managed it.

1. **Be Present in the Moment**: Empathy requires you to be fully present with the person you're interacting with. This means putting away distractions, like your phone or other tasks, and focusing on the conversation at hand. When you're fully engaged, the other person feels valued and understood, which enhances your ability to connect on an empathetic level.

Empathy in Leadership and Professional Settings

In professional environments, empathy is often viewed as a "soft skill," but it's one of the most impactful qualities a leader can have. Leaders who lead with empathy create supportive, collaborative work cultures where team members feel heard, respected, and motivated. This, in turn, leads to higher levels of job satisfaction, better performance, and reduced turnover.

For example, when managing a team, an empathetic leader will take the time to understand the unique challenges each team member faces. They might offer flexible work arrangements to accommodate personal needs or provide additional resources to help someone manage their workload. By doing so, they build a loyal, engaged team that's more likely to go the extra mile.

Moreover, empathy enhances communication in professional settings. Whether you're negotiating with a client, working through a conflict with a coworker, or providing feedback to an employee, empathy allows you to approach the situation with understanding and care. It fosters a sense of collaboration rather than confrontation, leading to more productive outcomes.

The Long-Term Impact of Empathy

Developing empathy isn't just about improving relationships with others; it's about becoming a more compassionate, understanding person overall. As you practice empathy, you'll find that it enriches your interactions, deepens your connections, and allows you to navigate complex emotional situations with greater ease.

Empathy also promotes emotional well-being. When you approach the world with empathy, you create an environment of support and connection, both for yourself and for those around you. This leads to stronger, more fulfilling relationships and a greater sense of satisfaction in both your personal and professional life.

Ultimately, cultivating empathy is one of the most valuable investments you can make in your emotional intelligence. It enhances your ability to connect with others, fosters mutual understanding, and equips you to handle life's challenges with grace and compassion. By prioritizing empathy, you'll not only elevate your emotional intelligence but also enrich every aspect of your life.

Emotional Regulation: The Key to Managing Your Emotions

While empathy is essential in understanding the emotions of others, emotional regulation is the critical counterpart that allows you to manage your own emotions effectively. Emotional regulation is the ability to stay in control of your feelings and reactions, especially during challenging or stressful situations. It's about navigating your emotional landscape with intention, ensuring that your emotions don't overwhelm you or lead to impulsive, regrettable actions.

Emotional regulation doesn't mean suppressing or denying your emotions. Instead, it involves acknowledging them, understanding their root causes, and responding in a way that aligns with your values and goals. By mastering emotional regulation, you not only enhance your emotional intelligence but also improve your relationships, decision-making, and overall mental well-being.

Understanding the Importance of Emotional Regulation

Emotions are powerful forces that shape how we perceive and respond to the world around us. They influence our thoughts, behaviors, and interactions with others. When we're able to regulate our emotions, we gain the ability to pause, reflect, and choose our responses rather than being driven purely by emotional impulses.

In both personal and professional settings, emotional regulation is a vital skill. Consider moments of conflict or high stress—these are the times when emotional regulation becomes especially important. Without it, emotions like anger, frustration, or anxiety can cloud your judgment and lead to rash decisions or heated arguments. On the other hand, by managing your emotions effectively, you can approach challenges with a calm and clear mindset, making thoughtful decisions even in high-pressure situations.

Emotional regulation also fosters resilience. Life is filled with unexpected setbacks and obstacles, but how you respond to these moments determines your long-term success and well-being. Emotional regulation allows you to bounce back from disappointments and face adversity with a positive, solution-oriented attitude.

The Science Behind Emotional Regulation

At its core, emotional regulation is about managing the interplay between the emotional and rational parts of your brain. The amygdala, located in the brain's limbic system, is responsible for processing emotions like fear, anger, and stress. When triggered, the amygdala can cause an immediate emotional reaction—often referred to as the "fight or flight" response.

However, the brain's prefrontal cortex, responsible for higher-order thinking, can step in to evaluate the situation more rationally. Emotional regulation occurs when you give your prefrontal cortex the time and space to take over, allowing you to process your emotions in a more balanced way.

This process is often referred to as "taking a pause" or "taking a breath." When emotions rise, giving yourself a moment to pause can make all the difference between reacting impulsively and responding thoughtfully.

Strategies for Strengthening Emotional Regulation

Just like empathy, emotional regulation is a skill that can be developed and strengthened with practice. Here are some practical strategies to help you build emotional regulation in your daily life:

1. **Practice Mindfulness**: Mindfulness is one of the most effective tools for emotional regulation. By staying present and aware of your emotions as they arise, you can observe them without immediately reacting. Mindfulness encourages you to notice how emotions manifest in your body—such as tension, a racing heart, or shallow breathing—and helps you slow down before making decisions.

You can practice mindfulness through meditation, breathing exercises, or simply by taking a few moments throughout the day to check in with your emotions. When you feel a strong emotion, pause and take a few deep breaths. This simple act can calm your nervous system and give you time to reflect before responding.

1. **Reframe Negative Thoughts**: Our emotions are often triggered by the way we interpret events around us. When

something negative happens, it's easy to fall into patterns of catastrophizing or assuming the worst. Emotional regulation involves challenging these negative thought patterns and reframing them in a more constructive light.

For example, instead of thinking, "This is a disaster; I'll never recover," you might reframe the situation as, "This is a setback, but I've faced challenges before, and I'll find a solution." Reframing allows you to shift your focus from the problem to potential solutions, reducing emotional overwhelm.

1. **Identify Your Triggers**: Emotional regulation is much easier when you're aware of your emotional triggers—those situations or people that tend to provoke strong reactions. Once you've identified your triggers, you can work on developing strategies to manage them.

For instance, if you know that certain work meetings tend to leave you feeling stressed or frustrated, you can prepare by practicing calming techniques beforehand or setting boundaries that protect your emotional well-being. Being proactive about managing triggers helps you maintain control over your emotions, even in difficult situations.

1. **Develop Healthy Coping Mechanisms**: Everyone experiences negative emotions from time to time, and emotional regulation involves finding healthy ways to cope with those feelings. Unregulated emotions can lead to unhealthy coping mechanisms, such as avoidance, overreacting, or numbing emotions with substances or distractions.

Instead, focus on developing positive coping strategies that allow you to process emotions without being consumed by them. Physical exercise, journaling, talking to a trusted friend, or engaging in a creative hobby are all examples of healthy outlets for emotions. These activities provide a constructive way to release emotional tension and regain a sense of calm.

1. **Cultivate Self-Compassion**: Emotional regulation also requires being kind to yourself, especially in moments of emotional struggle. It's natural to experience a wide range of emotions, and self-compassion allows you to acknowledge those feelings without judgment. Instead of criticizing yourself for feeling angry, anxious, or sad, offer yourself understanding and patience.

Self-compassion doesn't mean avoiding responsibility for your actions—it simply means treating yourself with the same kindness and forgiveness you would offer a friend in a similar situation. By practicing self-compassion, you create a more supportive internal environment that fosters emotional growth and resilience.

The Role of Emotional Regulation in Professional Settings

In professional settings, emotional regulation is a highly valued skill, especially for leaders and managers. Work environments can be stressful and fast-paced, and the ability to stay composed and level-headed under pressure sets you apart as someone who can handle challenges with grace.

For example, in a high-stakes negotiation, emotional regulation allows you to maintain control over your emotions, keeping you focused on achieving a positive outcome rather than reacting to frustrations or provocations. Similarly, in team settings, emotional regulation helps you manage conflicts, provide constructive feedback, and lead with empathy.

Employees and colleagues also look to leaders who demonstrate emotional regulation as models of emotional intelligence. A leader who can navigate stress without losing their composure sets the tone for the entire team, fostering a culture of calm, rational decision-making even in difficult situations.

Conclusion: Emotional Regulation as a Lifelong Practice

Emotional regulation is a lifelong practice that requires ongoing attention and refinement. While it may take time to develop, the benefits are profound. By mastering emotional regulation, you gain the ability to respond thoughtfully to life's challenges, maintain balance during stressful times, and build stronger, more harmonious relationships with others.

Ultimately, emotional regulation enhances not only your emotional intelligence but also your overall quality of life. It empowers you to live with greater emotional freedom, clarity, and resilience, ensuring that you remain in control of your emotions rather than being controlled by them.

{ 12 }

Chapter 12: Embracing Continuous Learning

The Value of Lifelong Learning

In a world that is constantly evolving, embracing lifelong learning is no longer a luxury—it's a necessity. The rapid advancement of technology, shifting economic landscapes, and ever-changing societal norms require us to continuously update our knowledge and skills if we are to remain relevant and successful. But beyond mere survival, lifelong learning offers a path to deeper personal fulfillment and professional growth. It is the key to unlocking new opportunities, expanding our horizons, and reaching our full potential.

Lifelong learning isn't about sitting in a classroom or earning a degree—it's about maintaining a sense of curiosity and an eagerness to explore the world around us. The most successful individuals are those who remain open to new ideas, who never stop asking questions, and who recognize that learning can come from a variety of sources. Books, podcasts, online courses, mentors, or even casual conversations with colleagues can all serve as catalysts for growth.

For many, the idea of continuous learning might seem daunting. After all, the demands of everyday life—work, family, social obligations—can make it difficult to prioritize personal development. However, lifelong learning doesn't have to be overwhelming. It's about developing a habit of seeking knowledge in manageable, consistent ways. For example, setting aside 20 minutes a day to read about a topic that interests you or signing up for a short online course can make a significant difference over time.

The benefits of lifelong learning extend far beyond career advancement. On a personal level, learning stimulates the brain, keeping it active and engaged. Studies have shown that continuous learning can improve cognitive function, reduce the risk of dementia, and even enhance emotional well-being. When we learn something new, we are challenged to think in new ways, which can boost creativity and problem-solving abilities.

Professionally, those who commit to continuous learning are more likely to be seen as adaptable, resourceful, and forward-thinking. In a competitive job market, these are the qualities that can set you apart from others. Employers value employees who take initiative in developing their skills and staying current with industry trends. Whether you're seeking a promotion, a new job, or just greater satisfaction in your current role, investing in your own development is one of the best moves you can make.

In today's fast-paced world, standing still is not an option. Industries evolve, new technologies emerge, and what was relevant yesterday may not be relevant tomorrow. By cultivating a mindset of lifelong learning, you not only future-proof yourself against these changes but also position yourself for greater success and satisfaction in both your personal and professional life.

So, where do you start? It begins with acknowledging that there's always something new to learn, regardless of your age, experience, or current level of expertise. Lifelong learning is about humility and curiosity. It's about recognizing that the world is vast and that there is always more to discover. Whether it's picking up a new hobby, diving into a new subject matter, or simply reflecting on past experiences to extract lessons from them, the value of lifelong learning cannot be overstated. When you commit to learning as a way of life, you open the door to endless possibilities for growth, enrichment, and success.

Developing a Growth Mindset

One of the most powerful ways to embrace continuous learning is by cultivating a growth mindset. A term popularized by psychologist Carol Dweck, a growth mindset is the belief that abilities, intelligence, and talents can be developed over time through effort, learning, and persistence. It contrasts sharply with a fixed mindset, where individuals believe their qualities are set in stone, unchangeable, and limited.

A growth mindset is fundamental to continuous learning because it encourages us to view challenges, setbacks, and even failures as opportunities to grow. Instead of seeing obstacles as roadblocks, those with a growth mindset see them as stepping stones. This perspective opens the door to personal and professional transformation, making it easier to adapt to new situations and acquire new skills.

The difference between a growth mindset and a fixed mindset can be seen in how we respond to failure. People with a fixed mindset often fear failure because they see it as a reflection of their abilities. For them, making a mistake is synonymous with being "not good enough." This belief leads to avoidance of challenges and a reluctance to step outside their comfort zone, ultimately stunting their growth. On the other hand, those with a growth mindset understand that failure is not the end but merely a part of the learning process. They embrace mistakes, understanding that each one brings valuable lessons that help them improve.

Consider a child learning to ride a bike. A child with a fixed mindset might give up after falling a few times, thinking, "I'm just not good at this." But a child with a growth mindset will see each fall as an opportunity to learn how to balance better next time. They understand that persistence, not natural talent, will ultimately help them master the skill. The same applies to adults in all areas of life—whether you're learning a new skill at work, developing a new habit, or facing a personal challenge, adopting a growth mindset will help you persist in the face of adversity.

One of the most empowering aspects of a growth mindset is that it allows you to focus on effort rather than outcomes. In a fixed mindset, people often fixate on results, believing that if they're not immediately successful, they never will be. But with a growth mindset, the emphasis is on the process—on learning, improving, and growing over time. Success, then, becomes less about achieving a specific goal and more about the journey toward continual self-improvement.

Developing a growth mindset doesn't happen overnight, but it is a skill you can nurture. Start by reframing how you talk to yourself in moments of challenge. Instead of saying, "I can't do this," try, "I can't do this yet." That single word—yet—signals to your brain that learning and growth are possible. When faced with setbacks, ask yourself, "What can I learn from this?" and, "How can I do better next time?" This kind of self-questioning leads to a deeper understanding of your own potential and encourages resilience in the face of obstacles.

Another strategy to foster a growth mindset is to seek out challenges deliberately. Take on tasks that push you beyond your comfort zone, knowing that even if you don't succeed immediately, you are building your skills and expanding your capabilities. Over time, you'll start to see that challenges are not something to be feared, but rather opportunities to stretch yourself in new ways.

Finally, surround yourself with people who model a growth mindset. Whether they are friends, colleagues, or mentors, being in an environment where curiosity, effort, and persistence are valued will help reinforce these qualities in yourself. Engage in conversations where you can learn from others' experiences, especially when they share stories of how they overcame challenges and grew through adversity.

A growth mindset is a powerful tool for personal and professional development. It allows you to face challenges with optimism, embrace failure as part of the learning process, and view your abilities as constantly evolving. By adopting this mindset, you open the door to continuous learning, empowering yourself to become more resilient, adaptable, and successful in all areas of life.

Learning Through Reflection

One of the most overlooked yet essential components of continuous learning is reflection. In our fast-paced world, we often move from one task to the next without pausing to consider what we've learned along the way. However, taking time to reflect on past experiences—both successes and failures—can deepen your understanding and provide invaluable insights for future growth. Reflection allows us to examine our actions, thoughts, and decisions, helping us identify patterns, recognize opportunities for improvement, and gain clarity about our goals.

Reflection is not just about looking back on what has happened; it's about asking meaningful questions that help you understand why things unfolded the way they did. Did you achieve a desired outcome? If so, what strategies worked, and how can you replicate that success? If not, what went wrong, and how can you approach similar situations differently in the future? By engaging in reflective practice, you transform everyday experiences into learning opportunities that shape your future behavior.

There are many ways to engage in reflection, and the method you choose should align with your personal preferences. One of the most effective techniques is journaling. Writing down your thoughts, feelings, and experiences allows you to explore them more deeply and objectively. You don't need to write long entries—just a few sentences about a significant event, how you felt about it, and what you learned can be incredibly illuminating. Over time, these journal entries become a record of your growth, showing you how far you've come and providing insights into the recurring themes of your life.

Consider reflecting on both your successes and your failures. It's easy to focus on mistakes and dwell on what went wrong, but it's equally important to examine what you've done well. Reflecting on your successes helps reinforce positive behaviors and gives you a clearer understanding of the strategies and mindset that led to favorable outcomes. By acknowledging your strengths, you gain confidence in your abilities and are more likely to replicate successful actions in the future.

Failures, on the other hand, are often the greatest teachers—if we let them be. When reflecting on a failure, it's essential to approach it with a mindset of curiosity and learning rather than judgment or self-blame. Ask yourself, "What could I have done differently?" or "What external factors contributed to this outcome, and how can I mitigate them next time?" This kind of critical self-reflection can turn painful experiences into stepping stones for growth, enabling you to approach future challenges with greater wisdom and resilience.

Another way to incorporate reflection into your life is by engaging in regular self-assessments. Periodically review your progress toward your goals and assess whether your actions align with your values and objectives. Are you moving in the direction you want to go? If not, why? Reflection helps you course-correct and make necessary adjustments to stay on track with your vision for personal and professional growth.

It's also helpful to seek feedback from others as part of your reflective process. Often, we are too close to our own experiences to see them clearly. Trusted friends, mentors, or colleagues can provide valuable perspectives on our actions and decisions, offering insights we may have missed. By listening to constructive feedback and reflecting on how it aligns with your own perceptions, you gain a more well-rounded understanding of your strengths and areas for improvement.

Finally, make reflection a regular habit, not just something you do after significant events or setbacks. Daily or weekly reflection can be a powerful tool for continuous learning. Set aside a few minutes at the end of each day or week to review what you've learned, what challenges you faced, and how you overcame them. Over time, this practice will sharpen your self-awareness, helping you make more informed decisions and grow both personally and professionally.

Reflection turns experience into insight, and insight into action. It is through this process that we truly learn from our lives, constantly refining our approach and becoming better versions of ourselves. When you take the time to reflect, you not only learn from your past but also create a roadmap for future success, making continuous growth an integral part of your journey.

Embracing a Growth Mindset

At the heart of continuous learning is the belief that your abilities and intelligence are not fixed—they can grow and evolve with effort, persistence, and learning. This belief, known as a "growth mindset," is a powerful driver for personal and professional development. When you embrace a growth mindset, you understand that challenges are not obstacles to avoid but opportunities to learn, and that failure is not a sign of incompetence, but rather a stepping stone toward mastery.

A growth mindset stands in stark contrast to a "fixed mindset," where individuals believe their talents and intelligence are set in stone and cannot be developed further. People with a fixed mindset often shy away from challenges, fearing that failure will expose their limitations. They may avoid trying new things, take criticism personally, and feel threatened by the success of others. In contrast, those with a growth mindset see effort as the path to improvement. They welcome challenges, see failures as temporary setbacks, and view constructive feedback as a valuable tool for learning.

To embrace a growth mindset, it's important to shift your perspective on effort and challenges. Instead of viewing effort as a sign that you're not naturally talented, recognize it as a key component of growth. Every time you work through a problem or push yourself to learn something new, your brain is building new connections, strengthening your abilities over time. This is the essence of neuroplasticity—the brain's ability to change and adapt in response to learning and experience. No matter how skilled you are today, you can become more skilled tomorrow with consistent effort and practice.

One practical way to adopt a growth mindset is to reframe how you talk to yourself, especially in challenging situations. Instead of saying, "I'm not good at this," try saying, "I'm not good at this yet." The simple addition of the word "yet" opens up the possibility of improvement and reinforces the idea that growth is possible. Similarly, when you encounter failure, instead of thinking, "I've failed," try reframing it as, "This didn't work, but what can I learn from it?" Shifting your internal dialogue from one of limitation to one of possibility helps foster resilience and a willingness to keep pushing forward.

Another key aspect of a growth mindset is embracing the power of feedback. People with a fixed mindset often struggle with receiving feedback because they perceive it as a threat to their self-worth. However, feedback is an essential component of growth—it provides insight into areas you may not be aware of and offers specific guidance on how to improve. To truly benefit from feedback, approach it with an open mind. Rather than feeling defensive or disheartened, see feedback as a tool to help you reach your potential. Remember that the goal is not perfection but continuous improvement, and feedback is one of the most valuable resources for achieving that.

In addition to being open to feedback, it's also essential to cultivate curiosity. A growth mindset thrives on curiosity—curiosity about new subjects, different perspectives, and innovative ways of solving problems. When you maintain a curious attitude, you remain open to learning from all experiences, whether they're inside or outside of your comfort zone. Curiosity keeps your mind engaged, helps you adapt to change, and allows you to explore new possibilities with enthusiasm rather than fear. It transforms learning from a chore into an exciting journey of discovery.

It's also important to recognize that adopting a growth mindset doesn't mean you'll never experience self-doubt or frustration. These emotions are natural, especially when you're learning something new or facing a difficult challenge. The key is to push through these moments, using them as fuel for growth rather than reasons to quit. People with a growth mindset understand that mastery takes time, effort, and persistence. They don't give up when the going gets tough—they dig deeper, seek out resources, and use setbacks as opportunities to learn and grow.

Finally, remember that adopting a growth mindset is a life-long process. It's not something you achieve overnight or check off a list. Instead, it's an ongoing commitment to seeing yourself as a work in progress, always capable of learning and improving. By continually challenging yourself, seeking feedback, and maintaining curiosity, you'll build resilience, adaptability, and a deeper sense of fulfillment in both your personal and professional life. Growth is not just an outcome—it's a mindset, a journey, and a way of living that will lead to greater success and satisfaction over time.

In embracing a growth mindset, you unlock your potential to learn and grow continuously, regardless of where you start. It becomes the driving force behind your journey of self-improvement, allowing you to navigate challenges, learn from failures, and achieve your goals with greater confidence and clarity.

Lifelong Learning: Cultivating Curiosity and Adaptability

Lifelong learning is the cornerstone of continuous growth, both personally and professionally. In a world that is constantly changing, the ability to learn, adapt, and evolve is what sets successful individuals apart. To cultivate lifelong learning, it is essential to nurture curiosity and embrace change as a natural part of the journey.

Curiosity is the fuel that drives learning. It's what pushes you to explore new topics, ask questions, and seek out knowledge in areas you may not have considered before. People who are curious are never content to stop at surface-level understanding—they dig deeper, ask "why," and look for connections between different ideas. This insatiable desire to learn keeps them constantly evolving, adapting to new trends, technologies, and challenges in their personal and professional lives.

One way to foster curiosity is by making a habit of asking questions. When you encounter something you don't understand, instead of shying away from it, approach it with a mindset of discovery. Ask yourself, "What can I learn from this?" or "How can this challenge help me grow?" This simple shift in perspective can turn even the most daunting tasks into opportunities for learning and self-improvement. By staying open to new experiences and information, you develop a broader understanding of the world around you and gain the ability to apply that knowledge in creative and impactful ways.

Another critical aspect of lifelong learning is the ability to adapt to change. In today's fast-paced world, change is inevitable, and those who resist it often find themselves left behind. Whether it's a shift in your career, new technology, or changes in your personal life, adaptability is key to maintaining relevance and continuing to grow. Lifelong learners understand that change isn't something to fear but rather a chance to learn something new, improve existing skills, or even discover new passions.

Adapting to change requires a willingness to step outside your comfort zone. While it's natural to seek security in routine, it's in the moments of discomfort where the most significant learning occurs. When you push yourself to try something unfamiliar—whether it's learning a new skill, taking on a challenging project, or engaging with people who have different perspectives—you expand your capabilities and become more resilient in the face of future changes. Lifelong learners thrive in environments where they are constantly exposed to new ideas and challenges because they see these experiences as opportunities to grow.

One of the most powerful tools for fostering lifelong learning is reading. Books, articles, and research papers open doors to worlds of knowledge that you may not encounter in your daily life. Reading allows you to dive into the minds of experts, philosophers, and innovators, giving you access to decades, if not centuries, of accumulated wisdom. Set a goal to read regularly—whether it's a book a month, an article a day, or even just 10 minutes before bed. The key is consistency. Over time, the knowledge you gain from reading will compound, providing you with a wealth of insights and ideas that you can apply to your personal and professional endeavors.

In addition to reading, seek out other learning opportunities that challenge you. Take online courses, attend workshops, or engage in mentorship programs. These structured learning environments provide a framework for growth, helping you gain new skills and knowledge in a focused and deliberate way. They also provide a sense of accountability, as they often involve deadlines, assessments, or feedback, all of which can motivate you to stay on track and continue progressing.

It's also important to recognize that learning doesn't have to be formal. Some of the most profound lessons come from life itself—from your interactions with others, the challenges you face, and even the mistakes you make. Every experience holds the potential for growth, and it's up to you to extract the lessons from it. Reflect on your experiences regularly. What went well? What could you have done differently? How can you apply what you've learned moving forward? By making reflection a regular part of your life, you'll become more self-aware and better equipped to navigate future challenges.

Finally, lifelong learning requires a commitment to never becoming complacent. It's easy to fall into the trap of thinking that you've learned enough or that you've reached the peak of your abilities. However, the moment you stop learning is the moment you stop growing. Even the most accomplished individuals in any field continue to push themselves to learn more, to stay curious, and to remain open to new ideas. They understand that mastery is a journey, not a destination, and that there is always more to learn, more to explore, and more to achieve.

Incorporating lifelong learning into your life not only enhances your personal growth but also keeps you adaptable and relevant in an ever-changing world. By cultivating curiosity, embracing change, and staying committed to learning, you set yourself up for continuous growth and success in all areas of your life. Learning becomes a habit, a mindset, and ultimately, a way of living that enriches your experiences and broadens your horizons.

{ 13 }

Chapter 13: Finding Work-Life Balance

Understanding the Importance of Work-Life Balance
In today's fast-paced world, the idea of work-life balance can often feel elusive, even unattainable. With the constant pressure to perform at our best in the workplace, coupled with personal obligations, it's easy to see why so many people struggle to strike the right balance. However, finding a healthy equilibrium between work and personal life is not only important—it's essential for long-term well-being, success, and happiness.

At its core, work-life balance is about managing your time and energy in a way that allows you to meet the demands of your job while still having time for personal activities, relationships, and self-care. It's not just about cutting back on work hours or spending more time with family; it's about creating harmony between the two aspects of your life in a way that aligns with your goals and values. When you achieve this balance, you are better able to function at your best both professionally and personally.

One of the most significant dangers of ignoring work-life balance is burnout. Burnout doesn't happen overnight—it's the result of prolonged stress, overwork, and neglect of personal needs. It can lead to physical exhaustion, emotional fatigue, and mental overwhelm. People who experience burnout often feel disconnected from their work, lose their passion, and struggle to maintain relationships. In the long run, burnout can have severe consequences for your health, leading to issues like anxiety, depression, high blood pressure, and even heart disease.

On the other hand, when you prioritize work-life balance, you create space for rest, relaxation, and rejuvenation. This not only enhances your physical and mental well-being but also makes you more productive and focused when you are at work. Research consistently shows that employees who take regular breaks, engage in hobbies, and spend quality time with loved ones are more creative, energized, and effective in their jobs. They are also less likely to make mistakes, have higher job satisfaction, and stay with their companies longer.

But work-life balance is not just a professional issue—it also impacts your personal life. When your work takes up too much of your time, it can strain relationships with family and friends. You may find yourself missing important events, neglecting your partner, or being too exhausted to engage in meaningful conversations. This can lead to feelings of guilt, frustration, and isolation, further increasing stress levels. In contrast, when you make time for the people you care about, your relationships deepen and thrive, providing emotional support that helps you navigate the challenges of work and life.

It's important to note that work-life balance is not about dividing your time equally between work and personal life. For most people, there will be periods when work demands more of your time, and other times when personal life takes priority. The key is to be mindful of how your time and energy are being distributed and to make adjustments when things start to feel off balance. Work-life balance is about being intentional with your time and making sure that both your professional responsibilities and personal needs are being met in a way that allows you to feel fulfilled and energized.

Ultimately, understanding the importance of work-life balance is the first step toward creating a life that is both productive and personally enriching. By acknowledging the need for balance, you can begin to make conscious choices that prevent burnout, nurture your relationships, and ensure that you are taking care of both your career and your personal well-being. This foundational awareness sets the stage for deeper exploration into how to achieve and maintain balance in the coming points.

Identifying Personal Priorities and Values

Finding work-life balance starts with a clear understanding of your personal priorities and values. Without this clarity, it's easy to get swept away by the demands of work and external expectations, leaving little room for the things that truly matter to you. By identifying what is most important in your life—whether it's family, health, career growth, or personal fulfillment—you can make more intentional decisions about how to allocate your time and energy.

We all have different priorities. For some, career success is a top priority, driving them to spend long hours in the office or invest significant time in developing their skills. For others, family or personal relationships take center stage, making time with loved ones a non-negotiable part of their daily routine. There's no right or wrong answer when it comes to your personal priorities—what matters is that you are clear on what they are and that they reflect your true values, not what society or others expect of you.

One of the most effective ways to identify your personal priorities is through self-reflection. Take some time to ask yourself the following questions:

- What areas of my life bring me the most joy and fulfillment?
- Which activities or relationships give me energy, and which ones drain it?
- If I had more time or resources, where would I choose to invest them?
- What are the things I would regret not doing or pursuing if I looked back on my life?

These questions can help you gain clarity on what is truly important to you. Often, we assume we know our priorities, but when we take a step back and reflect, we realize that our actions don't always align with them. For example, you might say that your family is your top priority, but if you're constantly working late and missing important family events, there's a disconnect between your stated values and your behavior. Identifying this gap is the first step toward realigning your life in a way that reflects your true priorities.

Once you have a clear sense of your priorities, it's important to define your core values. Values are the guiding principles that influence your decisions, actions, and how you show up in the world. They help you determine what's right or wrong for you and provide a framework for making decisions that feel authentic and meaningful. Examples of core values include integrity, compassion, creativity, success, and personal growth. Understanding your values helps you create a life that is not only balanced but also aligned with who you are at your core.

For instance, if one of your core values is personal growth, you might prioritize learning and self-improvement in your daily routine. This could involve setting aside time for reading, taking courses, or engaging in new experiences that challenge you. On the other hand, if your value is family connection, you might prioritize quality time with loved ones, making sure to carve out space for activities that strengthen those relationships.

Another crucial aspect of identifying priorities and values is understanding that they can change over time. What mattered most to you five years ago may not be as important today. Life transitions, such as starting a family, changing careers, or moving to a new place, often cause a shift in what we value. As you navigate different stages of life, it's important to regularly reassess your priorities and values to ensure that your actions continue to align with what matters most to you.

Incorporating your priorities and values into your daily life doesn't happen overnight—it requires conscious effort and reflection. But once you have clarity on what's important to you, decision-making becomes easier. You can say "no" to opportunities or obligations that don't align with your values without guilt, and you'll feel more confident in how you spend your time. The pursuit of work-life balance will feel less like a struggle and more like a natural extension of living a life that is aligned with your deepest priorities and values.

Setting Boundaries to Protect Your Time

One of the most essential strategies for achieving work-life balance is setting clear and firm boundaries. In today's world, where work can often seep into every corner of our lives—thanks to technology, constant communication, and increasing demands—learning to establish and maintain boundaries is not just a skill but a necessity. Without boundaries, it's easy to become overwhelmed, overworked, and burnt out, leaving little room for the personal and professional fulfillment you seek.

Setting boundaries starts with recognizing that your time is finite and valuable. Time is the one resource you can never get back, and every minute you spend on something that doesn't align with your priorities is a minute you can't devote to what matters most. To protect your time, you must be deliberate about where and how you invest it. This involves making intentional choices about when to say "yes" and, more importantly, when to say "no."

Many people struggle with saying "no," whether it's to colleagues, supervisors, friends, or even family members. They fear disappointing others, missing out on opportunities, or being perceived as uncooperative. However, constantly saying "yes" to every request, task, or commitment often leads to a lack of balance and, eventually, burnout. The key is understanding that every "no" is really a "yes" to something else—usually something that aligns more closely with your personal values and priorities.

To set effective boundaries, start by identifying the areas in your life where you feel stretched too thin. Are there specific work tasks that consistently take up more time than they should? Do you find yourself constantly responding to emails or phone calls outside of your designated work hours? Is your personal time often interrupted by work-related matters, leaving you with little space to unwind or connect with loved ones? These are the areas where boundaries need to be established.

Once you've identified where you need boundaries, it's important to communicate them clearly and assertively. If you're trying to protect your evenings for personal time, for instance, let your colleagues know that you won't be responding to work emails after a certain hour. If you need uninterrupted time during the day for focused work, inform your team that you'll only be available during specific hours for meetings or conversations. Clarity is key. The more transparent you are about your boundaries, the easier it will be for others to respect them.

Another critical aspect of boundary-setting is learning to manage expectations—both your own and others'. Sometimes, the pressure to overcommit comes from our internal beliefs that we must always be available, productive, or responsive to every demand. Letting go of the need for constant availability can be liberating. You don't have to attend every meeting, respond to every email within minutes, or be the first to volunteer for every project. Setting realistic expectations for yourself and others helps ensure that your boundaries are respected.

It's also important to recognize that boundaries aren't just about saying "no" to others—they're also about saying "yes" to yourself. This means giving yourself permission to take breaks, to disconnect from work when necessary, and to prioritize activities that recharge and rejuvenate you. Whether it's scheduling regular time for exercise, hobbies, family, or even relaxation, setting personal boundaries around your well-being is crucial for maintaining a healthy work-life balance.

Of course, setting boundaries is not a one-time event—it's an ongoing process. As your responsibilities shift or as you enter different stages of life, your boundaries may need to be adjusted. For instance, you might need stricter boundaries during particularly busy seasons at work or more flexibility during periods of personal change, like starting a family or caring for a loved one. The key is to remain flexible and responsive to your evolving needs while maintaining a firm commitment to honoring your own time and well-being.

In addition to setting boundaries, enforcing them is equally important. It's easy to set a boundary but much harder to uphold it, especially when faced with resistance or pushback. There will be moments when others may not immediately respect your boundaries, either out of habit or because they're used to your previous availability. In these situations, it's essential to remain consistent. Politely remind others of your boundaries and resist the temptation to cave in to pressure. Over time, people will come to respect the lines you've drawn, and you'll begin to experience the benefits of a more balanced life.

Ultimately, setting boundaries is an act of self-respect. It demonstrates that you value your time, your well-being, and your personal priorities enough to protect them. When done effectively, boundaries not only help you achieve work-life balance but also empower you to show up more fully and authentically in all areas of your life. You'll find that you have more energy, focus, and fulfillment, both personally and professionally, simply by guarding your most precious resource—your time.

Point 4: Prioritizing Self-Care for Long-Term Balance

In the quest for work-life balance, self-care often takes a backseat. Many people view it as a luxury or something they'll focus on "later"—after work deadlines are met, household chores are done, or family obligations are taken care of. But the truth is, self-care is not a luxury; it's a necessity for sustaining balance, energy, and overall well-being. Without it, you can easily fall into patterns of exhaustion, overwhelm, and burnout, ultimately diminishing your ability to perform well both personally and professionally.

At its core, self-care is about acknowledging your own needs and giving yourself permission to meet them. It involves taking regular, intentional steps to nourish your physical, mental, and emotional health. For some, self-care might look like taking time for physical exercise, whether it's a daily walk, yoga class, or trip to the gym. For others, it might mean setting aside time for relaxation, meditation, or pursuing hobbies that bring joy and fulfillment. The important thing to remember is that self-care isn't one-size-fits-all—it's highly personal and should be tailored to what works best for you.

One of the biggest obstacles to prioritizing self-care is the mindset that it's selfish or indulgent. Many people, especially those who juggle work, family, and other responsibilities, feel guilty for taking time for themselves. However, this mindset is not only counterproductive but also harmful. Self-care is about replenishing your own energy reserves so that you can show up more fully in every area of your life. Without proper care and attention to your well-being, you risk depleting yourself, which not only impacts your own quality of life but also diminishes your capacity to care for others and excel in your professional roles.

In fact, research consistently shows that individuals who make time for self-care are more productive, creative, and resilient. When you prioritize your own health and happiness, you're better equipped to handle stress, solve problems, and navigate challenges. Self-care helps to reduce stress hormones, improves mood, and promotes better sleep—three key factors that directly influence your ability to perform at your best. By taking regular breaks to recharge, you can return to your work and personal tasks with greater focus, energy, and a clearer perspective.

Another critical aspect of self-care is managing stress. In today's fast-paced world, stress can feel inevitable. Whether it's the pressure to meet deadlines, the demands of family life, or the constant flow of information and communication, stress can easily overwhelm even the most organized person. Learning how to manage and mitigate stress is essential to maintaining balance.

This can be achieved through practices like mindfulness, meditation, and relaxation techniques that help calm the mind and reduce tension in the body.

Mindfulness, in particular, has gained widespread recognition for its ability to improve focus and reduce stress. By staying present and fully engaged in the moment, you can avoid the mental clutter that often contributes to feelings of overwhelm. Even just a few minutes of mindfulness meditation each day can make a significant difference in how you handle daily challenges. Additionally, mindfulness allows you to become more aware of your emotional and physical needs, enabling you to respond to stressors in a healthier, more constructive way.

Sleep is another essential component of self-care that is often neglected in the pursuit of work-life balance. It's easy to sacrifice sleep to meet deadlines, answer emails, or catch up on tasks, but chronic sleep deprivation can have serious consequences on both your mental and physical health. Sleep is the time when your body repairs itself, your brain processes information, and your emotions reset. Without adequate rest, your cognitive function, decision-making abilities, and emotional resilience are significantly impaired. Prioritizing sleep—aiming for at least seven to eight hours a night—should be non-negotiable for anyone seeking balance and long-term well-being.

Self-care also extends to nurturing your emotional health. This means giving yourself space to process your feelings, reflect on your experiences, and cultivate emotional awareness. Journaling, talking to a trusted friend or therapist, and engaging in activities that bring you joy are all ways to support your emotional well-being. Emotions are a natural part of life, and suppressing or ignoring them can lead to greater stress and imbalance over time. By taking care of your emotional health, you not only improve your overall happiness but also strengthen your ability to cope with challenges and setbacks.

Ultimately, the key to effective self-care is consistency. It's not about indulging in occasional acts of pampering but about integrating small, daily habits that support your overall well-being. By making self-care a priority, you are investing in your long-term health and happiness. It's important to remember that self-care doesn't have to be time-consuming or expensive; it can be as simple as taking a few minutes each day to breathe deeply, stretch, or enjoy a quiet moment of reflection. The goal is to create a sustainable routine that fits into your life and allows you to recharge regularly.

In the context of work-life balance, self-care serves as the foundation upon which everything else is built. Without it, you may find yourself constantly struggling to keep up, feeling drained, and ultimately unable to sustain the balance you desire. By prioritizing self-care, you give yourself the energy, clarity, and resilience needed to manage the demands of both your personal and professional life. Remember, you can't pour from an empty cup—taking care of yourself ensures that you have the capacity to give to others and achieve success in all areas of your life.

Point 5: Setting Boundaries to Protect Your Time and Energy

One of the most critical yet challenging aspects of achieving work-life balance is setting and maintaining boundaries. In a world where we are constantly connected—where emails, texts, and calls can reach us at any hour—it's easy to blur the lines between work and personal life. Without clear boundaries, your time and energy can be consumed by the demands of others, leaving you feeling drained, overwhelmed, and perpetually on the verge of burnout.

Setting boundaries is not about saying "no" to everything or isolating yourself from responsibilities. Rather, it's about defining clear limits that allow you to protect your time, energy, and well-being. Boundaries help you establish a healthy balance between work and personal life, ensuring that neither area suffers at the expense of the other. When done effectively, boundaries allow you to focus on what matters most, create time for rest and relaxation, and avoid the pitfalls of overcommitting.

The first step in setting boundaries is recognizing where your time and energy are currently being spent. Take an honest inventory of your daily schedule. Are you frequently working late into the evening? Do you find yourself saying "yes" to tasks or requests that leave you feeling resentful or exhausted? Are you sacrificing personal time—such as exercise, family activities, or hobbies—because of work demands? These are all signs that your boundaries may need to be adjusted.

Once you've identified the areas where boundaries are needed, the next step is to communicate them clearly and assertively. This can be particularly challenging in professional settings, where there may be pressure to always be available or to take on extra work. However, it's essential to remember that setting boundaries is not a sign of weakness or a lack of commitment—it's a strategy for maintaining long-term productivity and well-being.

For example, if you're finding that work is consistently spilling over into your evenings, you might set a boundary of not answering work-related emails after a certain time each day. If you're being asked to take on more tasks than you can reasonably manage, you can communicate your capacity and suggest alternative solutions or timelines. It's important to be clear and direct when setting boundaries, ensuring that others understand your limits and respect them.

In addition to setting boundaries with others, it's equally important to set boundaries with yourself. This includes recognizing your own tendencies to overwork, procrastinate, or neglect self-care in favor of productivity. Often, the most difficult boundaries to enforce are the ones we set for ourselves. For instance, if you've decided to dedicate an hour each day to exercise or personal hobbies, it's crucial to honor that commitment just as you would a meeting or work deadline. By holding yourself accountable to your own boundaries, you reinforce the importance of balance in your life.

Another essential component of setting boundaries is learning how to manage your time effectively. Time management and boundaries go hand in hand; without the ability to prioritize and organize your time, even the most well-intentioned boundaries can quickly erode. This means developing habits like scheduling blocks of time for focused work, minimizing distractions, and creating a routine that allows for breaks and downtime. By managing your time wisely, you create space for both work and personal life to coexist in a way that feels balanced and fulfilling.

It's also important to recognize that setting boundaries is not a one-time event—it's an ongoing process that may require adjustments as your circumstances change. For example, during particularly busy seasons at work, you may need to temporarily adjust your boundaries to accommodate deadlines or projects. The key is to remain flexible and self-aware, ensuring that any temporary shifts don't become permanent habits that undermine your balance.

One of the most significant challenges people face when setting boundaries is dealing with guilt or fear of judgment. You may worry that by setting limits, you'll be perceived as uncooperative, lazy, or not a team player. However, the reality is that people who set clear boundaries are often more respected and valued because they demonstrate a strong sense of self-awareness and the ability to manage their time effectively. By taking care of your own needs, you're better able to show up fully in your work and relationships, which ultimately benefits everyone.

It's also worth noting that boundaries can look different for different people. Some may need strict boundaries around their work hours, while others might need to set limits on social commitments, technology use, or household responsibilities. The important thing is to determine what works best for you and to communicate those boundaries clearly to others. This might mean having conversations with your boss about expectations, discussing responsibilities with your family, or even setting limits on your own phone or computer use.

In the end, setting boundaries is about creating a life that feels balanced, sustainable, and aligned with your values. It's about protecting your time and energy so that you can focus on the things that matter most—whether that's spending quality time with loved ones, pursuing personal passions, or excelling in your career. By setting and maintaining clear boundaries, you take control of your life, prevent burnout, and ensure that you have the capacity to thrive both personally and professionally.

As you continue your journey toward work-life balance, remember that boundaries are not walls meant to shut others out—they are frameworks that allow you to protect and nurture yourself, so that you can show up fully and meaningfully in all areas of your life.

Chapter 14: Sustaining Motivation and Momentum

Understanding the Nature of Motivation

Motivation is the invisible force that drives action, but its nature can be elusive and, at times, difficult to sustain. At its core, motivation comes in two forms: intrinsic and extrinsic. Intrinsic motivation comes from within—it's the internal desire to do something because it's personally rewarding. It's driven by passion, purpose, or enjoyment. Extrinsic motivation, on the other hand, stems from external rewards like money, praise, or recognition. While both types are powerful, intrinsic motivation tends to fuel long-lasting drive and satisfaction, while extrinsic motivation may offer short-term bursts that fizzle out once the reward is attained.

To harness motivation effectively, it's essential to first understand why you're pursuing a specific goal. This means connecting with your "why"—the deeper reason behind what you're trying to achieve. For example, if you're working toward a promotion at your job, the external reward may be a pay raise or a new title, but your intrinsic motivation could be a desire for personal growth, leadership opportunities, or a sense of accomplishment. Understanding this distinction is crucial because, when the external rewards lose their appeal or become out of reach, your intrinsic motivation will keep you moving forward.

Take some time to reflect on what truly drives you. What do you value most? Is it freedom, creativity, family, or the opportunity to make an impact on others? When you align your goals with your core values, motivation becomes a natural extension of your purpose. This alignment creates a powerful internal compass that guides you, especially when challenges arise or progress feels slow. Without this deeper connection, it's easy to become discouraged when faced with obstacles or setbacks.

However, motivation is not a constant. Even when you're deeply connected to your purpose, you will experience fluctuations in your drive. Some days, you'll feel energized and ready to tackle anything; other days, you might struggle to take even the smallest step forward. This ebb and flow are natural. The key to sustaining motivation through these periods of fluctuation lies in maintaining awareness of your purpose and adjusting your strategies as needed.

A helpful practice to stay connected to your motivation is to frequently revisit your "why." Whether it's through journaling, meditation, or simple reflection, regularly ask yourself: "Why is this important to me?" When you feel disconnected or unmotivated, reminding yourself of your deeper purpose can reignite your passion and help you push through the tough days.

Another factor to consider is that motivation thrives on progress. Human beings are wired to find satisfaction in movement, in seeing incremental improvement. This is why it's important to set both long-term goals and short-term milestones. The feeling of accomplishment, no matter how small, reinforces your intrinsic drive and encourages you to keep going. Each milestone achieved becomes evidence that you're capable of success, and this builds momentum over time.

In essence, motivation is a dynamic and multi-faceted force that requires both internal reflection and external action. By understanding the difference between intrinsic and extrinsic motivation and staying connected to your deeper purpose, you can cultivate a source of energy that not only pushes you toward your goals but also sustains you through the inevitable ups and downs along the way.

Setting Achievable and Incremental Goals

Once you've connected with your deeper sense of purpose, the next critical step in sustaining motivation is learning how to set achievable and incremental goals. Grand ambitions can be exciting and inspiring, but without breaking them down into manageable steps, they can quickly become overwhelming. This is where the power of incremental progress comes in. Setting small, measurable goals that lead toward your larger objectives not only builds momentum but also makes the journey toward success feel more attainable.

The key to setting effective goals lies in the SMART framework—Specific, Measurable, Achievable, Relevant, and Time-bound. This method ensures that your goals are not only clear but also realistic and actionable. Let's break down each component:

- **Specific**: Your goal needs to be clear and precise. For example, instead of saying "I want to get fit," say "I want to lose 10 pounds in three months by exercising three times a week and following a healthy eating plan." The more specific you are, the easier it is to visualize and plan for success.
- **Measurable**: It's important to have a way to track your progress. This allows you to see how far you've come and

provides tangible evidence of your efforts. In the fitness example, you can measure progress through weekly weigh-ins, body measurements, or tracking the number of workouts completed.

- **Achievable**: Goals should challenge you, but they also need to be realistic. Setting a goal that's too far out of reach can lead to frustration and burnout. Ask yourself: Is this goal something I can reasonably accomplish with the resources and time I have available?
- **Relevant**: Your goals should align with your larger purpose. If a goal doesn't contribute to your long-term vision, it's easy to lose motivation. Ensure that each goal fits into the bigger picture of what you're trying to achieve.
- **Time-bound**: Every goal needs a deadline. A sense of urgency helps drive action and prevents procrastination. Without a timeline, goals can drag on indefinitely, and the momentum that comes from steady progress will fade.

For instance, if your long-term goal is to start your own business, you might feel overwhelmed by the scope of what needs to be done. However, by applying the SMART framework, you can break this larger goal into smaller, more achievable tasks. Your specific goal might be, "I will develop a business plan within the next two months." This goal is measurable because you can check your progress weekly as you build different sections of the plan. It's achievable because two months is a reasonable time frame. It's relevant because it directly contributes to your ultimate aim of starting the business. Finally, it's time-bound with a clear deadline for completion.

Breaking down big dreams into smaller, manageable goals doesn't just make the path forward clearer—it also provides opportunities to celebrate progress. Celebrating small wins is crucial for maintaining motivation. Every time you achieve a milestone, no matter how small, you reinforce the belief that you are capable of reaching your larger goal. These small victories serve as a reminder of the progress you're making, and each step forward fuels your drive to keep going.

In addition, setting incremental goals creates a sense of momentum. Each small accomplishment propels you into the next task, and before you know it, you've built a rhythm of success. Motivation thrives on movement, and nothing keeps you moving forward more effectively than the tangible results you see from taking consistent action.

By setting achievable and incremental goals, you're not only creating a clear path toward success, but you're also giving yourself the opportunity to experience the satisfaction of progress along the way. These small steps, when strung together, lead to significant, lasting change. And as you accomplish each goal, your motivation grows stronger, helping you sustain the energy and focus needed to reach your ultimate destination.

Cultivating a Growth Mindset

Sustaining motivation and momentum over the long term requires more than just clear goals—it requires the right mindset. One of the most powerful tools for maintaining motivation is cultivating a growth mindset. This concept, popularized by psychologist Carol Dweck, suggests that individuals with a growth mindset believe that their abilities and intelligence can be developed through dedication and hard work. In contrast, those with a fixed mindset believe that their abilities are innate and unchangeable.

The difference between these two mindsets is striking. With a fixed mindset, challenges and setbacks are seen as failures or indications of personal inadequacy. This can quickly lead to discouragement and giving up. However, with a growth mindset, challenges are viewed as opportunities for learning and improvement. Instead of feeling defeated by obstacles, individuals with a growth mindset are motivated to work harder and find creative solutions to overcome them.

One way to foster a growth mindset is by reframing how you view failure. Instead of seeing failure as something negative, try to view it as a valuable learning experience. Every setback or mistake is a chance to grow and improve. Ask yourself: "What can I learn from this situation?" and "How can I use this experience to get better?" Shifting your focus from the outcome to the process of learning can significantly impact your ability to stay motivated in the face of challenges.

For example, imagine you're working toward a goal of advancing in your career, but you face a setback—perhaps you didn't get the promotion you were hoping for. A fixed mindset might interpret this as a sign that you're not good enough or that you're stuck where you are. On the other hand, a growth mindset would encourage you to reflect on what you can learn from the situation. You might ask, "What skills can I develop to be a stronger candidate next time?" or "How can I improve my performance in areas that were mentioned in feedback?" This shift in perspective helps you remain motivated, even when things don't go according to plan.

A key aspect of the growth mindset is embracing challenges. Often, we are tempted to stay in our comfort zones, where success feels guaranteed and failure seems distant. However, real growth happens when we step outside of what is familiar and face challenges head-on. By actively seeking out new experiences that push your limits, you develop resilience and the ability to overcome obstacles. This, in turn, builds confidence in your ability to handle future challenges, keeping your motivation high.

Another way to cultivate a growth mindset is by focusing on effort rather than inherent talent. People with a fixed mindset often believe that success is the result of natural ability, which leads them to give up when they encounter difficulties. In contrast, a growth mindset emphasizes the importance of effort and persistence. Recognizing that improvement comes through hard work allows you to remain motivated, even when progress is slow.

Consider athletes, for example. Top performers in any sport are not born with all the skills they need to succeed. They may have some natural ability, but they spend countless hours practicing, refining their techniques, and pushing themselves to improve. What sets them apart is their commitment to continuous effort. By applying the same mindset to your personal and professional goals, you can keep moving forward, knowing that each step—no matter how small—brings you closer to success.

Finally, to develop a growth mindset, surround yourself with people who encourage and inspire you to keep growing. The environment you create for yourself has a significant impact on your mindset and motivation. Seek out mentors, friends, or colleagues who embody the growth mindset and who can provide support when you're faced with challenges. Engaging in conversations with people who value learning and persistence can help reinforce your own belief in your ability to grow.

By embracing the growth mindset, you shift your focus from perfection to progress. This perspective makes it easier to stay motivated over the long term, as you come to see every experience—whether positive or negative—as an opportunity to learn and grow. Rather than being discouraged by setbacks, you use them as fuel to propel you forward. In doing so, you not only sustain your motivation but also cultivate the resilience needed to achieve lasting success.

Leveraging Small Wins for Lasting Momentum

Sustaining motivation over the long haul can often seem daunting, especially when you're working toward big, ambitious goals. The key to maintaining momentum is learning how to leverage small wins along the way. Small wins, or incremental achievements, provide vital psychological fuel that keeps you moving forward, even when the ultimate destination feels far away.

The power of small wins lies in their ability to create a sense of progress. When you're working toward a larger goal, it can be easy to get overwhelmed by the scale of the task. This is particularly true if you're only focused on the final outcome—something that might be months or even years in the future. Without regular reinforcement of progress, your motivation can falter, leading to procrastination or even abandonment of the goal altogether.

Breaking a larger goal into smaller, manageable tasks allows you to celebrate these mini-achievements. Each time you complete one of these tasks, you get a psychological boost—a sense of accomplishment that reaffirms your ability to succeed. This concept, sometimes referred to as "the progress principle," suggests that making consistent, incremental progress toward a meaningful goal is one of the most effective ways to maintain a high level of motivation.

For example, imagine you're writing a book—a project that could take several months. If you focus only on completing the entire book, it's easy to feel overwhelmed. However, if you break that larger goal into smaller milestones, like writing a chapter a week, you can celebrate each chapter as a victory. Each small win reassures you that you're on the right track and capable of completing the project, keeping your momentum high.

Small wins also help build confidence. Each time you achieve one, it reinforces your belief in your ability to succeed. This self-assurance is critical when facing setbacks or challenges. When you have a series of small victories behind you, it becomes easier to push through difficulties because you have evidence of past success. You can look back and say, "I've already achieved X, Y, and Z, so I can handle this next step too."

Another way to leverage small wins is by tracking your progress. Whether it's through a journal, a spreadsheet, or an app, visually seeing your progress can be incredibly motivating. Many people find that simply checking off completed tasks creates a sense of satisfaction that helps keep them moving forward. These small moments of recognition can compound over time, creating a steady flow of positive reinforcement that sustains motivation.

For instance, if you're trying to lose weight, tracking each pound lost can provide that boost of motivation you need to keep going. Even if the final goal is to lose 30 pounds, seeing that you've lost 5 or 10 already reminds you that your efforts are paying off. It reinforces the idea that progress is happening, even if it's not immediate or dramatic. The same applies to financial goals, career milestones, or personal development—tracking small wins makes your journey feel more tangible and achievable.

In addition to tracking your progress, it's important to consciously celebrate your small wins. These celebrations don't need to be grand; they can be as simple as treating yourself to something special, taking a break, or sharing your success with a friend or loved one. Acknowledging your accomplishments, no matter how small, strengthens your motivation to continue working toward the larger goal.

For instance, if you're working on a major professional project, like launching a business, you can set smaller milestones—developing a business plan, securing funding, or creating a marketing strategy. As you achieve each one, take a moment to recognize the progress you've made. These celebrations act as powerful psychological rewards, reinforcing the behavior that led to the achievement and motivating you to push toward the next milestone.

Small wins are also crucial when facing setbacks. Often, when things don't go according to plan, it's tempting to focus on what went wrong and lose sight of the progress you've made. In these moments, reflecting on your small wins can help restore your confidence and provide the encouragement needed to keep moving forward. They remind you that, despite temporary setbacks, you are still making progress toward your goals.

Finally, small wins contribute to creating positive habits. When you focus on consistent, small achievements, you build a routine of success. Over time, this routine becomes ingrained, making it easier to sustain momentum without requiring as much effort or motivation. The small wins create a feedback loop where success leads to more success, fueling your motivation and helping you stay committed to your long-term goals.

In summary, small wins provide both the psychological and practical reinforcement needed to keep going when faced with large, ambitious goals. They break down overwhelming tasks into achievable steps, boost confidence, and create a sense of ongoing progress. By consistently celebrating these small victories, you'll find it easier to maintain momentum and stay motivated, no matter how long the journey may take.

Cultivating Long-Term Vision for Sustainable Success

While small wins keep you motivated day to day, cultivating a long-term vision is essential for sustaining momentum over the long haul. A compelling vision acts as a guiding star, helping you stay focused on the bigger picture, even when distractions, challenges, or setbacks threaten to pull you off course.

Your long-term vision is more than just a goal—it's the deeper "why" behind what you're striving for. It's the overarching purpose that gives meaning to your efforts and drives your persistence. Without a clear vision, it's easy to lose motivation once the initial excitement of a new project or pursuit fades. But with a strong vision in place, you have a reason to keep pushing forward, even when the going gets tough.

A long-term vision provides clarity and direction. When you know where you're headed, it becomes easier to map out the path to get there. This allows you to set more specific, achievable goals that align with your vision. Whether in your personal or professional life, having a clear sense of purpose enables you to prioritize the activities and tasks that will bring you closer to realizing your vision, while filtering out distractions that don't serve your larger goals.

For example, if your long-term vision is to build a successful business that helps people live healthier lives, every decision you make—from the products you create to the partnerships you pursue—can be evaluated against that vision. When an opportunity arises, you can ask yourself, "Does this align with my vision?" If it does, it's worth pursuing. If it doesn't, you can confidently pass, knowing it would only detract from your ultimate goal.

One of the biggest challenges to sustaining motivation over time is maintaining enthusiasm when progress seems slow or obstacles arise. A long-term vision helps you weather these difficult periods because it reminds you of what you're working toward and why it matters. Even when the day-to-day grind feels exhausting, your vision keeps you connected to the broader impact you're striving to make.

Consider the example of an aspiring writer. The process of writing a book can take months, if not years, and it's easy to get discouraged along the way. However, if the writer has a clear vision of why they're writing—whether it's to inspire others, share valuable knowledge, or fulfill a personal dream—that vision becomes a source of inspiration when the writing process gets tough. It reminds them that the temporary discomfort of writer's block or fatigue is worth pushing through because the ultimate goal is meaningful.

Creating a long-term vision requires reflection and self-awareness. You need to connect with your core values and identify what matters most to you. Start by asking yourself questions like, "What kind of life do I want to create?" or "What impact do I want to have on the world?" Your answers to these questions will help you shape a vision that resonates with your personal and professional aspirations.

Once you've defined your vision, it's important to revisit it regularly. Just as you track your small wins to stay motivated, reviewing your long-term vision keeps you aligned with your broader purpose. Life has a way of throwing curveballs, and it's easy to get sidetracked by short-term pressures or new opportunities that seem appealing in the moment. However, consistently reflecting on your vision allows you to course-correct when necessary and ensure that your actions remain in line with your overarching goals.

It's also essential to be flexible with your vision. While it's important to have a clear direction, your vision isn't set in stone. As you grow, learn, and evolve, your vision may shift. What matters is that it continues to reflect your core values and passions. Being open to refining your vision as circumstances change allows you to stay true to yourself while adapting to new opportunities and challenges.

A long-term vision not only helps you stay focused, but it also fuels intrinsic motivation. Unlike external rewards—like praise, money, or recognition—intrinsic motivation comes from within. It's the satisfaction and fulfillment you derive from working toward something that matters deeply to you. When you're intrinsically motivated, you're less reliant on external validation, and more resilient in the face of setbacks.

For example, if your vision is to become a leader in your industry, that internal drive will keep you motivated to continually learn, grow, and push yourself to the next level. The satisfaction you feel from working toward that vision—knowing that each step brings you closer to becoming the person you aspire to be—will sustain your momentum, even when external rewards aren't immediately forthcoming.

A powerful vision also creates a ripple effect in your life. It influences your mindset, your habits, and the way you show up each day. When you're connected to a long-term vision, you're more likely to make decisions that are aligned with your goals. You'll choose persistence over giving up, growth over comfort, and long-term rewards over short-term gratification.

In conclusion, cultivating a long-term vision is essential for sustaining motivation and momentum on your journey toward success. It gives you clarity, purpose, and direction, allowing you to navigate challenges with greater resilience. A compelling vision keeps you focused on the big picture, while your small wins provide the motivation to take the necessary steps along the way. By continuously aligning your actions with your vision, you ensure that your efforts are moving you toward the life and career you truly want to create.

Conclusion: Your Journey to Elevation

Reflecting on Your Personal and Professional Growth
As you come to the end of this book, take a moment to reflect on the journey you've undertaken. Personal and professional growth is not a one-time achievement but an ongoing process that requires consistent self-awareness and introspection. Think back to the very first chapter, where you began with the fundamental question: "What is my purpose?" It's possible that, at the start, the idea of finding purpose felt daunting or abstract. Now, with each chapter explored and each point reflected upon, you've likely gained a clearer sense of who you are, what drives you, and how you want to shape your life.

The first step in this reflection is to acknowledge the areas where you've already grown. Maybe you've learned to identify and challenge limiting beliefs that held you back, or perhaps you've adopted new habits that promote resilience and positivity. Take stock of these shifts—no matter how small they may seem—because they mark the beginning of meaningful change. Growth often comes in small, incremental steps, and it's easy to overlook progress when we are focused solely on the larger goals.

Asking the right questions has been a core theme throughout this book, and here, in this moment of reflection, it's time to ask yourself a few more:

- How have my beliefs about myself changed since I started reading this book?
- What actions have I taken to align my daily life with my core purpose?

- What new skills or habits have I started to develop, and how have they impacted my life?

These questions are designed to help you recognize how far you've come. Often, we are so caught up in our pursuit of success and improvement that we forget to celebrate the small victories along the way. But these small victories are what form the foundation of sustained growth.

It's also important to acknowledge the challenges you've faced throughout this process. Growth doesn't happen without discomfort or resistance. You've likely encountered moments when you had to confront limiting beliefs, change old habits, or step outside your comfort zone. Reflect on those moments—how did you handle them? What did you learn about yourself in the process? Each challenge you've faced has given you valuable insight and strength.

Finally, look at how your personal and professional life have started to align. Often, we think of personal growth and career success as separate paths, but as this book has shown, they are deeply interconnected. As you develop greater self-awareness and emotional intelligence, you enhance your ability to succeed in your career. Similarly, as you set and achieve professional goals, you build confidence and reinforce your personal growth.

This reflection is not just about looking back, but about preparing for the next steps. Growth doesn't stop here. The insights and strategies you've gained are tools you can continue to use, refining and adapting them as your life evolves. Each phase of your journey will bring new challenges, but it will also offer new opportunities for reflection, learning, and growth.

The key to this journey is recognizing that it's not about perfection; it's about progress. And now, as you take stock of where you've been, you are better equipped than ever to move forward with clarity and purpose.

Embracing the Process of Continuous Growth

One of the greatest realizations you can take from this journey is that growth is not a destination, but a process. Often, we think of personal and professional development as a series of milestones—achieving a promotion, mastering a skill, or reaching a particular goal. While these milestones are significant, they represent only moments along a lifelong path of evolution. True growth is continuous, requiring ongoing effort, learning, and self-reflection.

At this stage, you've likely gained a deeper understanding of the importance of embracing the process rather than fixating solely on the outcomes. When you focus on the process, you allow yourself to enjoy the journey, to appreciate the lessons learned along the way, and to be more present in your day-to-day life. It's easy to get caught up in the pursuit of external success, but as you've explored throughout this book, success is most meaningful when it aligns with your internal values and personal fulfillment.

Embracing continuous growth means being open to learning at every stage of life. It's about maintaining a mindset that is flexible, curious, and resilient. You've learned that setbacks and challenges are not signs of failure, but opportunities for growth. Each time you face adversity—whether in your personal life or your career—you have a choice: to retreat and remain stagnant or to adapt, learn, and move forward stronger than before.

This is where the power of a growth mindset comes into play. A fixed mindset, as you've discovered, limits your potential. It convinces you that your abilities and intelligence are set in stone, leading to a fear of failure and a reluctance to try new things. On the other hand, a growth mindset allows you to see challenges as opportunities to expand your capabilities. It fosters resilience, persistence, and an eagerness to embrace new experiences.

As you continue on your path of growth, it's important to regularly ask yourself key questions that encourage this mindset:

- How can I learn from the challenges I'm facing right now?
- What new skills or knowledge can I acquire to enhance my personal and professional life?
- How can I stay adaptable in the face of change?

These questions keep you in a state of curiosity, pushing you to seek out new opportunities for development. They remind you that no matter how much you achieve, there is always room to learn more, improve, and evolve.

A significant part of embracing continuous growth is also about letting go of perfectionism. Perfectionism often leads to frustration, burnout, and disappointment because it sets an unrealistic standard that no one can consistently meet. By focusing on progress over perfection, you allow yourself the freedom to experiment, make mistakes, and grow from those experiences. You begin to see that imperfections are not flaws, but essential parts of the learning process.

Remember, growth is rarely linear. There will be moments of rapid advancement, as well as periods of slower progress or even temporary setbacks. These fluctuations are natural, and they don't diminish the value of the journey. What matters most is your commitment to showing up, staying open to learning, and continuously seeking ways to elevate yourself.

By embracing this process, you cultivate a sense of purpose that goes beyond any individual achievement. You come to understand that the journey itself is what makes life rich and meaningful. Each step forward, no matter how small, brings you closer to a fuller, more authentic version of yourself.

Aligning Your Actions with Your Values

As you move forward on your journey of growth, one of the most important lessons is learning how to align your actions with your values. This alignment is key to living a life of purpose, fulfillment, and authenticity. Without it, you may find yourself pursuing goals that look impressive on the outside but leave you feeling empty and disconnected on the inside.

When your actions reflect your values, you experience a sense of congruence—a harmony between who you are, what you believe, and what you do. This alignment not only strengthens your personal integrity but also gives you the energy and motivation to keep moving forward. It becomes your guiding compass in both your personal and professional life, helping you make decisions that are true to yourself, even when faced with external pressures or expectations.

So, how do you ensure that your actions consistently align with your values?

The first step is clarifying what your core values are. Values are deeply held beliefs that guide your decisions and shape your behavior. They reflect what matters most to you—whether it's integrity, compassion, creativity, financial independence, or family. Often, we have a general sense of our values but haven't taken the time to articulate them clearly. By identifying your core values, you create a foundation upon which to build your life.

Take a moment to reflect on the following questions:

- What principles guide your decisions?
- What makes you feel most fulfilled or proud?
- When do you feel most at peace or aligned with yourself?

Once you have clarity on your values, the next step is to evaluate how closely your daily actions reflect those values. This is where the real work begins. It's one thing to know your values intellectually; it's another to live them out in your everyday life. For example, if one of your core values is family, but you're consistently working long hours with little time for loved ones, there's a disconnect that needs to be addressed. If you value creativity but find yourself stuck in a job that stifles innovation, you're likely to feel frustrated and unfulfilled.

Aligning your actions with your values often requires making changes—sometimes small, sometimes significant. These changes may involve setting boundaries, re-prioritizing your commitments, or even re-evaluating your career choices. This process can be challenging, especially when it requires stepping outside your comfort zone or letting go of things that no longer serve your purpose. But the rewards are profound. When you start living in alignment with your values, you'll notice a deeper sense of fulfillment, peace, and authenticity.

Another crucial aspect of aligning actions with values is accountability. It's easy to drift off course when life gets busy or when you face external pressures. This is why it's important to regularly check in with yourself and ask:

- Am I living in alignment with my values?
- Are there areas where I'm compromising or straying from what's important to me?
- What changes can I make to get back on track?

One effective way to stay aligned is through intentional goal-setting. When you set goals that are directly tied to your values, you create a roadmap for living a more purposeful life. Each goal becomes a reflection of what you truly care about, and every step you take towards achieving that goal brings you closer to living your values fully.

Finally, surrounding yourself with like-minded individuals who share or respect your values can help reinforce this alignment. The people you interact with daily—whether friends, family, or colleagues—can either support or undermine your efforts to live authentically. Choose to be around those who encourage you to stay true to yourself and who inspire you to continue growing in alignment with your values.

Aligning your actions with your values is not a one-time task; it's an ongoing process. Life will throw challenges and temptations your way, but when you are grounded in your values, you will have the clarity and strength to navigate these obstacles with integrity and purpose. This alignment is the key to unlocking lasting fulfillment, both personally and professionally, and it is one of the most powerful ways to elevate your life.

Embracing the Power of Adaptability

In the journey toward personal and professional growth, one of the most vital skills you can cultivate is adaptability. Life is dynamic, and the only constant is change. Whether it's in your career, relationships, or personal aspirations, unforeseen challenges and opportunities will inevitably arise. How you respond to these changes can either propel you forward or hold you back. By embracing adaptability, you can navigate life's twists and turns with resilience and grace, positioning yourself for continuous growth.

Adaptability is not about abandoning your goals or values; it's about being flexible in how you achieve them. It's the ability to pivot when circumstances demand it, without losing sight of your ultimate destination. When you cultivate adaptability, you develop a mindset that views change not as a threat, but as an opportunity for learning and growth. This perspective shift is empowering—it turns challenges into stepping stones and failures into valuable lessons.

One of the first steps in embracing adaptability is recognizing that plans rarely unfold exactly as anticipated. No matter how meticulously you plan, there will always be factors beyond your control—economic shifts, personal setbacks, or even shifts in your own desires and passions. When you accept that uncertainty is part of life, you free yourself from the rigidity that can hinder progress. Instead of resisting change, you learn to flow with it, making adjustments as needed while keeping your long-term vision intact.

For example, consider someone who sets out to start a new business. Their initial plan might focus on a specific market or product, but as they gather more information and receive feedback from potential customers, they might realize that the market is oversaturated or that their product doesn't meet consumer needs. A rigid mindset might lead them to persist with their original plan, even when it's clear that it's not working. However, an adaptable mindset would encourage them to pivot—perhaps targeting a new market, refining the product, or exploring an entirely new approach. By being flexible, they increase their chances of success, rather than clinging to a failing strategy.

Adaptability also requires a level of self-awareness and humility. It's essential to acknowledge when something isn't working and to be willing to change course without letting pride or fear of failure get in the way. This means letting go of the need for perfection and embracing a growth mindset—the belief that you can improve and evolve over time. When you see challenges as opportunities for learning rather than as obstacles, you become more resilient in the face of adversity.

Another aspect of adaptability is the ability to continually reassess your goals and methods. What worked for you five years ago might not be effective today, and what you value now might shift as you grow. Regularly reflecting on your progress, priorities, and strategies allows you to make informed adjustments that keep you aligned with your evolving aspirations. This ongoing process of evaluation and adaptation ensures that you remain relevant and effective, both personally and professionally.

In the professional world, adaptability is often seen as a key trait of successful leaders and innovators. Industries are constantly evolving, with new technologies, market trends, and customer demands emerging all the time. Those who can adapt quickly to these changes are the ones who thrive. They are not only able to survive in fluctuating environments, but they are also able to seize new opportunities and stay ahead of the curve. Whether it's learning new skills, adopting new technologies, or shifting strategies, adaptability allows professionals to stay agile in a competitive landscape.

On a personal level, adaptability also fosters stronger relationships. In any relationship—whether with a partner, family member, or friend—there will be times when you need to adjust your expectations, communicate differently, or compromise. Relationships that are too rigid can break under the pressure of change, but those that allow for flexibility and growth are more likely to endure. By embracing adaptability, you can navigate the inevitable ups and downs of life's interpersonal dynamics with greater ease and understanding.

Finally, adaptability leads to greater resilience. When you are adaptable, you are better equipped to bounce back from setbacks and challenges. Instead of being overwhelmed by difficulties, you learn to see them as temporary obstacles that can be overcome with time, creativity, and effort. This resilience, in turn, fuels your motivation to keep moving forward, no matter what life throws your way.

In summary, adaptability is a powerful tool for navigating change and uncertainty. By being open to new possibilities, adjusting your strategies as needed, and maintaining a growth mindset, you can continue to make progress toward your goals, even in the face of adversity. Embracing adaptability not only allows you to thrive in a rapidly changing world but also empowers you to turn challenges into opportunities for personal and professional elevation.

Cultivating a Growth Mindset for Lifelong Progress

As you continue on your journey of personal and professional growth, one of the most transformative mental shifts you can make is to cultivate a growth mindset. A growth mindset is the belief that your abilities, intelligence, and talents are not fixed, but can be developed through effort, learning, and perseverance. It's a fundamental outlook that encourages constant improvement and sees setbacks not as failures, but as opportunities to learn and grow.

At its core, a growth mindset is about embracing the belief that no matter where you start, you can always elevate your skills and knowledge. It's an empowering idea—one that helps you push beyond your current limits and break through the barriers that once seemed insurmountable. When you adopt this mindset, challenges become less daunting, because you begin to see them as part of the process of growth, not as roadblocks to your success.

One of the key characteristics of a growth mindset is the willingness to step out of your comfort zone. It's easy to stay within the boundaries of what you know, but true growth comes from pushing yourself to explore new areas, take risks, and embrace uncertainty. This could mean learning a new skill, taking on a challenging project at work, or seeking out opportunities that test your abilities. With a growth mindset, you approach these experiences with curiosity and excitement, knowing that even if you stumble, you'll learn something valuable along the way.

Consider a scenario in which you are presented with a new opportunity at work—a project that requires skills you haven't fully developed yet. If you have a fixed mindset, you might shy away from it, fearing that you'll fail or that others will see your weaknesses. But with a growth mindset, you'll approach it differently. You'll see it as a chance to stretch yourself, to grow into the role, and to develop the skills needed to succeed. Rather than fearing failure, you'll be motivated by the challenge and eager to improve. This shift in perspective changes how you tackle new situations and opens up new possibilities for personal and professional elevation.

Another aspect of cultivating a growth mindset is learning to view feedback as a tool for improvement rather than as criticism. Many people avoid feedback because it can feel like a personal attack on their abilities or self-worth. But with a growth mindset, you begin to see feedback as essential to growth. Whether it's praise, constructive criticism, or even difficult feedback, it provides you with valuable information about how you can improve. Instead of letting it diminish your confidence, you use it as a guide to refine your approach, adjust your strategies, and become better at what you do.

One of the most powerful aspects of a growth mindset is how it changes your relationship with failure. People with a fixed mindset tend to avoid failure at all costs because they see it as a reflection of their inherent abilities. But when you have a growth mindset, failure becomes a learning tool. It's no longer something to be feared or avoided—it's something to be embraced. Every failure holds within it the seeds of improvement, as long as you're willing to learn from it. This shift allows you to take more risks, try new things, and recover quickly when things don't go as planned.

The importance of perseverance cannot be overstated when it comes to a growth mindset. The journey to personal and professional growth is not a straight line, and there will be times when progress feels slow or difficult. It's easy to give up when the going gets tough, but a growth mindset encourages you to keep going, even when you face obstacles. It reminds you that growth is a long-term process, and that with enough effort and persistence, you will eventually reach your goals.

Additionally, cultivating a growth mindset is about fostering a love for learning. When you view life as a continual learning process, you become more open to new ideas, perspectives, and experiences. This intellectual curiosity drives you to seek out knowledge in all areas of your life—whether that's reading new books, taking courses, or learning from mentors and peers. This constant pursuit of learning not only expands your skills but also keeps you adaptable and relevant in a rapidly changing world.

One practical way to foster a growth mindset is by setting learning-based goals instead of outcome-based goals. Instead of focusing solely on the end result—such as achieving a certain promotion or hitting a specific milestone—set goals around the learning process itself. For example, you might set a goal to improve a particular skill or to gain knowledge in a specific area. This shifts your focus from immediate success to long-term growth and encourages continuous learning and development.

In conclusion, cultivating a growth mindset is a foundational element of personal and professional elevation. It shifts your perspective from one of limitations to one of possibilities, encouraging you to continually push your boundaries and embrace challenges with enthusiasm. By viewing failure as a stepping stone to success and feedback as a tool for improvement, you empower yourself to grow in ways you never thought possible. Ultimately, a growth mindset is what allows you to stay committed to lifelong progress, transforming every experience into an opportunity to elevate your life.